Trucking Business Startup

Step-by-Step Guide to Start, Grow and Run Your Own Trucking Company in as Little as 30 Days

Clement Harrison

By reading this document, the reader agrees that under no circumstances is the author responsible for any losses, direct or indirect, that are incurred as a result of the use of the information contained within this document, including, but not limited to, errors, omissions, or inaccuracies.

Your Free Gift

Want to finally turn your passion into profit and gain access to a roadmap on how to build your online store successfully?

Whether you decide to monetize your passion on the side or build a real business from what you love, you'll inevitably need an online presence.

I'd like to give you a gift as my way of saying thanks for purchasing this book. It's my 20-page PDF Action guide titled *The Online Store Game Plan: 8 Simple Steps to Create Your Profitable Online Business*

It's short enough to read quickly, but meaty enough to know the actionable steps to take when starting your online business

In *The Online Store Game Plan* you'll discover:

- How to create your online store in 8 simple steps
- 3 key pillars that will lay the foundations of your online success
- The perfect online business model for your company
- What online platform will suit your business
- Several ways to attract customers to your online store

And much more....

Scan the QR-Code Now to access *The Online Store Game Plan* and set yourself up for online success!

Table of Contents

Introduction

"Build your own dreams or someone else will hire you to build theirs."

- Farrah Gray

Do you fit any of the following descriptions?

- You're looking to start a home business but haven't figured out how.
- Looking for a business that you can start from home.
- Are interested in boosting your income?
- You're a truck driver tired of driving for others and want to go big and make money, plus own your time.
- You simply want to start your own business and be your own boss.
- Or you're a stay-at-home parent looking for the right business to start.

If one of the above describes you, then I have good news for you. Let me explain.

The United States has the third highest population in the world, with just over 328 million people. All these people are consumers. They are always lookig for something to eat and enjoy. Entertainment is a big component of life and Americans enjoy it. Now, there's one industry that ensures that American people get the bulk of what they consume. That industry is trucking.

And it currently transports over 72% of the freight in the U.S.

Why am I telling you this? The answer is simple. The trucking industry thrives because of small businesses. And you can join the bandwagon and enjoy a piece of this industry's cake worth over $700 billion. What's exciting is that anyone with the desire to get into this industry can do so because it has a low entry barrier.

So, if you've been wanting a business idea to start your venture, here's an opportunity. You may think that it's a disadvantage if you have no background in trucking. Like with anything in life, especially in the information age, it's quick to get up to speed with the right knowledge. And I'll show you in a moment what's inside this book to get started right.

In fact, people interested in starting a trucking business ask questions such as:

1. Can I start a trucking business without having to drive?
2. Is trucking a profitable business?
3. Do I need a lot of money to start a trucking business?
4. What are the risks of starting a trucking business?
5. How do I get a loan for my business?
6. Where do I find customers?
7. What permits do I need?
8. What laws should I know about?

If you have one or more of the above questions, then this book is for a person like you. As you read through the contents, you'll notice how easy it is to start a trucking company from scratch. You may not have a commercial driving license and are eager to get one, but this book covers that process.

Let me tell you what you'll learn throughout the book.

The key to winning in business is to start a business in an industry with a proven growth record. This metric assures you of ongoing business growth. With this in mind, Chapter 1 paints a clear picture of why you may be missing out on one of the best types of small businesses that you could start.

Importantly, you'll discover factors that influence the trucking business so that you can position your company for success, not failure.

Now, you may be wondering if trucking businesses are profitable. That's a legitimate concern, and I hear entrepreneurs worrying about their ventures often. It's no use running a business at a loss. You're in luck because you can operate a profitable trucking company for sure. However, you'll need to get four things right to become profitable.

New business owners often worry about start-up costs. Indeed, the trucking business requires you to have start-up capital, but you don't need to have vast amounts of cash stashed somewhere to start this kind of venture. I'll show you how to craft a business plan that improves your chances of getting funding. Above all, you'll learn the reasons behind trucking business failures. Armed with this knowledge, you'll defend yourself against the possibility of becoming a victim of business failure.

As you can guess, the trucking industry is unique. There are certain legal requirements that you'll need to meet. And they begin with ensuring that your business is legal. I'll explain the different kinds of entities that you could start, plus their pros and cons. Most importantly, this book will cover the various permits that your business needs. I do this for one reason: I want you to get started right so you can build your business on a solid foundation.

Once you have all the necessary paperwork in place, I'll take you through how to build your fleet of trucks. You'll understand the advantages and disadvantages of buying or leasing your trucks. You need the right truck ownership strategy to maximize your chances of success as a start-up. Above all, it's vital to select the right equipment for the kind of freight that you want to load and ship. Should you choose to buy your own trucks, that would be no problem at all! I'll walk you through the different financing opportunities.

A trucking business cannot succeed without good drivers. These drivers ensure that you deliver what you promise in the freight contracts. As long as you do what you say you'll do, customers will love your company, and they'll want to keep doing business with you. That's why I describe how to hire good truck drivers. Included are the criteria to look for while hiring. Most importantly, I will show you how to find the kind of customers you want for your business. This is crucial because customers bring cash to the company.

Another vital skill in business is negotiating. I've covered this so that you can use it to get high-paying freight loads and make more money.

Running a business can be intimidating if you aren't sure what and how to manage it. One vital aspect of sound business management involves managing finances. Entrepreneurs often dislike this part of the business. Hence, they mistakenly give it to bookkeepers or some accounting professionals. These experts are good at generating numbers but are not necessarily professional business managers. This is your job as a business owner.

That's why I show you the main accounting terms and financial statements so that you can be able to manage your business finances.

Not only will I show you the value of monitoring business expenses, I'll also take you behind the scenes and reveal how fuel taxes get calculated so that you can be strategic in how you buy fuel. A good fuel-buying strategy will go a long way in improving the profitability of your venture.

Perhaps you may be wondering what gives me the authority to write a book about the trucking business. It is my passion to help others succeed in life; I am a bestselling author and founder of a consultancy firm called Muze Publishing.

I come face to face with many entrepreneurs and people of all walks of life who want to free themselves from the 9 to 5. It pleases me when their lives turn for the better because of our advice. Because I focus on the fundamentals of business and personal success, my ideas are applicable in almost every industry.

What you're about to learn has helped people from many different backgrounds enjoy personal and business success. We've helped dozens of entrepreneurs start and build successful businesses with our books. And I decided to write this book to help people like you start their own successful trucking business. There's no doubt that small businesses carry a country like ours on their shoulders. For example, the proportion of small businesses in the trucking industry is around 91%. You can imagine the impact that these small businesses have on our country. And this trend appears throughout the world. I firmly believe that small businesses can change the world.

This book, *Trucking Business Startup*, is a way to feed you the right information and knowledge to start your own successful small business. Unlike others who start trucking businesses without setting the right foundations, you'll be different and improve your odds of success.

The journey to starting a trucking business begins with the first chapter that shows what the industry has to offer you. Go ahead and find out right away!

Chapter 1
Why a Trucking Business

To succeed in every business, including the trucking business, you need a regular flow of customers and income. This helps your business to stay afloat because it can afford to pay all its bills on time. For this to happen, it's necessary to enter a competitive industry with proven prospects of growth. Now, does the trucking industry in the United States meet these requirements? Let's dive into the industry and investigate.

Trucking companies play a vital role in moving different kinds of goods throughout the United States. Look around you for a moment. You own a refrigerator to cool and chill food and beverages so that they are tasty and stay fresh for longer. Have you ever given a thought to how it moved from the manufacturer to your home? The manufacturer had to transport it to a wholesaler, who in turn, hauled it to your local retailer. Then your local store brought it to you with a truck.

Take any other item in your home like your computer, bed, clothing, and windows and it got delivered to your home with a truck. So, truck companies play an enormous distribution role in the whole value chain from manufacturing to the consumption of goods. In 2019, trucks carried 72.5% (by weight) of all freight in the U.S. That's almost three-fourths of all the goods moved in just one year. In tonnage terms, 2019 saw this industry hauling 11.84 billion tons of goods (American Trucking Associations, n.d.).

This represents a tonnage growth of 1.04 or 9.63% from the 2017 freight weight of 10.8 tons (John, 2019). In 2017, the trucking industry moved around 70 percent of all freight in the U.S. As you can see, 2019 grew by about 2.5%. In absolute numbers, this is an incredible amount.

Furthermore, the trucking industry generated 791.7 billion U.S. dollars in 2019 (John, 2019). To put the size of this industry into perspective, its 2019 revenue is larger than the gross domestic product (GDP) of Bangladesh and many other countries. If the trucking industry were a country, it would rank 33rd going by GDP! On the employment front, the trucking industry hired around 7.4 million people. This represented 5.8% of all full-time employees in the U.S.

Imagine the industry stop working for a few days or a week! What do you think the impact would be throughout the country? Chaos. For example, stores would run out of food that citizens need to function normally. Other industries like construction, import and export would suffer greatly. In short, the country could stall. And life for most people would change completely. Experts predict that if trucks were to stop for three consecutive days, stores would run out of food. That's tragic for us as consumers, isn't it?

With a large chunk of revenue coming domestically, the trucking industry faces little exposure to direct foreign exchange fluctuations. This can give your trucking company stability, something that is crucial for planning and executing those plans.

The trucking industry often indicates the health of the U.S. economy. When the economy swings upwards, the industry's customers move more and more freight to meet consumer demand. On the other hand, a low trucking demand indicates the start of an economic downturn.

Outlook of the Trucking Industry

We have now looked at the current and past performance of the trucking industry. To complete the sustainability picture of the industry, we now look into the future. Yes, no one can predict the future, but we can have a good sense of what to expect in a few years to come with an understanding of the past.

Around mid-2018 the trucking industry reached a peak and then began an 18-month downturn. As a result, carriers saw decreased truck orders. As if that wasn't enough, insurance premiums increased. This put pressure on many trucking companies and led to increased bankruptcies.

Things began to improve soon after the downturn period and the outlook seems bright. Contract truckload volumes have increased by 27%, even during a period that normally declines (Della Rosa, 2020). You may be wondering what increased demand for trucks. You see, the government greatly stimulated our economy financially and increased the unemployment benefits. These interventions resulted in increased consumer spending. And the effect filtered through to the supply chain and positively impacted the trucking companies. As a result, truckload volumes have shot up by 25% compared to 2018 levels (Della Rosa, 2020).

This bodes well for the truck companies as industry experts expect contract rate negotiations to stay unchanged or increase in single digits. In addition, the capacity is tight and spot prices keep growing. The national load spot rates jumped 25% compared to 2019 levels (Della Rosa, 2020). With improving rates, carriers are likely to see higher profits and the timing couldn't be better to start a trucking business.

Just so you don't get confused, let me explain the difference between spot rates and contract rates. Spot rates are short-term truckload prices. Twenty percent of the trucking market comes from spot rates. In contrast, contract rates are long-term freight prices subject to either party's adjustments when they deem it necessary. This often occurs when the supply and demand equation changes. The remaining 80 percent of the freight market comes from these contract rates.

The next significant trucking business influencing factor is the ongoing truck driver shortage. Coupled with rising freight demand and increasing truckload prices, this situation paints a welcoming picture for new trucking businesses. In 2018, the trucking industry had a shortfall of about 900,000 qualified truck drivers (Raphelson, 2018). This means that the industry battled to cater to its market fully. Thus, trucking freight customers had to find other ways to get their goods delivered in time and cost-effectively to their destination.

This is an excellent opportunity for you to join the industry and help it meet customer trucking demands. Experts predict that conditions in the trucking industry will likely remain strong and gradually improve. In fact, these experts see the sector growing by 27% in the next 10 years! That's welcome news to a person like you. But there's more good news.

Small trucking companies dominate the trucking industry, with 91% of them running their businesses with six or fewer trucks (Corporation Service Company, n.d.). This indicates that you can get business in the industry even if you are a beginner. Now, if you empower yourself with the right knowledge and skills, you'll be able to reap extraordinary economic results in this industry. And you've already taken the first step in gathering the required knowledge and skills by purchasing this book.

Factors That Influence the Trucking Industry

It's essential to arm yourself with the right knowledge before starting any business. More importantly, you need to know those niggling issues that could derail your ambitions. The same applies to the trucking business. There are factors that every carrier owner should know and take into consideration in their strategic planning. Let's discuss seven of the most important factors.

1. **Supply of Truck Drivers**

   A trucking business cannot survive even a day without drivers. Truck driving is a demanding job because you can spend days away from home and far from friends. Then there are government regulations, the weather, and schedules that require a great deal of responsibility. Overall, the lifestyle of truck drivers doesn't appeal to many people. Earlier I shared that the U.S. trucking industry is in dire need of qualified drivers.

The aging of current drivers has exacerbated the situation even more. Furthermore, the industry is seeing dropping numbers of employees who choose truck driving as their profession. As a result, businesses battle to keep or find qualified truck drivers. This forces Trucking business owners to offer their drivers better salaries to keep them for longer or to attract new drivers.

This situation isn't ideal for a trucking business start up because it can lead to increased overhead and reduce its survival chances. You may wish to consider driving your own truck in the beginning if you're already qualified. If you prefer to hire drivers, your negotiation skills need to be sharp to avoid overpaying. Perhaps you might consider other benefits like stock options for your drivers instead of hiring them at large salaries.

2. **Fuel Cost**

Trucks run on diesel, a product of oil refining. For this reason, your fuel cost will be affected by the changing oil prices. The unfortunate thing is that a carrier has no control over the price of oil. High fuel prices force you to forward the cost to your customers to remain profitable. Unfortunately, you may become less price competitive and lose some customers. This may lead to running fewer trucks. And this is not good for a trucking business.

However, you can control, to a certain extent, the fuel efficiency of each truck in your fleet. Right from the beginning, you should work out the fuel efficiency that makes each truck profitable, and then control future fuel costs around that baseline figure. Of course, the way the driver operates the truck would influence fuel efficiency. Hence, having skilled drivers not only shields you from safety issues but can help keep your business running costs low as well.

3. **Market Changes**

When the U.S. economy grows, trucks' demand follows suit because more freight needs to be moved. The opposite is also true. This means that the trucking business is seasonal. For example, when the holidays approach, shipping activity generally increases in anticipation of higher consumer demand. As such, spot rates also increase, resulting in trucking businesses making more money.

4. **Weather Events**

Natural disasters, such as hurricanes and winter storms, can negatively impact the truck industry. During these times, it's challenging to drive and the number of loads delivered drops. This results in decreased revenues for affected trucking businesses. Weather delays can cost carriers somewhere between $2.2 to $3.5 billion annually. Unfortunately, as a trucking business owner you have no control over natural weather events.

5. **Changing Government Regulations**

As you'll learn in Chapters 2 and 3, a trucking company must comply with several groups of regulations, such as safety and tax. There are many government regulations and organizations that can potentially affect your carrier. Some of these government arms include the Department of Transportation (DOT), the Federal Motor Carrier Safety Administration (FMCSA), the Occupational Safety and Health Administration (OSH), the Department of Labor (DOL) and many other federal, state, and local regulatory agencies.

To keep up with all the necessary regulations costs money. And thus, changing regulations could affect your profitability.

6. **Carrier Capacity**

The factors I've discussed above can result in some trucking businesses filing for bankruptcy, especially the less established carriers. For example, when larger carriers raise driver salaries, smaller trucking companies tend to find it challenging to match their larger competitors' wages. As a result, these smaller companies lose drivers to larger carriers and face the inevitable: filing for bankruptcy.

7. **Theft or Loss**

Theft in the trucking industry occurs either internally or externally. Internal theft takes place when your own employees steal from you. On the other hand, external theft involves someone unlinked to your carrier.

Shippers prefer to hire truckers that always deliver their freight to target destinations. When your business is often a victim of theft, especially internally, your reputation suffers. And this can make it difficult for you to get business.

Another common form of internal theft is the stealing of fuel. Luckily, there are technologies to help you to prevent this loss. But if your own employees steal the goods that your business delivers, then you'll face a serious trust challenge from shippers. So, you'll need to have systems in place to prevent theft.

Those are some of the factors that could affect your trucking business. Now, I'd like to talk with you about the good and the bad of a trucking business.

The Pros of a Trucking Business

Everything created by humans has both pros and cons. So it is with a trucking business. Let's first look at the pros.

- **Independence**. When you're working for someone, you have limited decisions that you can make. Besides, you may have to pass your decisions by your boss for them to be implemented. But running your own trucking business allows you to make and implement your own decisions. One key decision that you have to make is which trucking niche to operate in. You may decide to support food manufacturers, construction companies or makers of electronics.

You're also free to choose the days of the week for work and the days when you're off. But you should know that the decisions you make and the control you have come with responsibility and accountability.

- **Flexibility**. Working for yourself provides more freedom than working for someone else. The reason is that you have the freedom to work on your own terms. You're free to run your own schedule. Furthermore, you depend far more on yourself to deliver the results that you promise your customers.

- **Profitability**. When working for another carrier, you earn a salary over which you have little control. But running your own carrier provides you with an opportunity to make more because you can generate a lot more profit. Most importantly, you can determine the level of profit per load you want because you set up the shipment contract and deliver the freight.

Let's now turn our attention to the cons of a trucking business.

The Cons of Running Your Own Carrier

Not all is rosy when running your own trucking company. Here are some challenges you'll likely face.

- **Time-consuming**. When driving for a large carrier, your main job is simply to drive and deliver the freights. An owner-operator or trucking business owner has a lot more to do. For example, you'll have to ensure that the business runs as smoothly as possible, obtain funding (if necessary), and ensure that the trucks' maintenance occurs without failure. Furthermore, you need to find customers and prepare contracts.

  So, you may not have much free time, especially in the beginning. However, suppose you resolve from the start to build systems for business operations like sales and marketing, operational procedures, safety procedures, and so on. In that case, you'll soon free up a lot of time.

- **Responsibility**. Owning and running your own trucking business comes with benefits. However, the perks mean that you have to be responsible for a lot more. If the business isn't finding customers, you'll have to figure out why and solve the problem. One vital area that you will need to be on top of is ensuring that you comply with all applicable government regulations.

- **Stress.** Starting any business from scratch isn't easy, let alone a trucking company in an industry with so many regulations. It can be tough to get good customers and the right load prices. In trucking, a carrier's reputation enhances the chances of becoming a profitable business. But being a start-up that lacks the reputation of an established business can be immensely stressful.

  Another strain-causing area is ensuring that you have the funds to run your business efficiently. So, you need to network intelligently to find the capital as well as profitable trucking loads to build your brand. Initially, you may have to learn new skills and this isn't a walk in the park.

- **High start-up costs.** Starting a trucking company can be capital-intensive because of the type of equipment you need to have. So, you may need to develop skills to find funds quickly. Luckily, there are financing options in the transportation industry to help you get started right. If you do your homework thoroughly, becoming your own boss can soon be a reality.

Now you have a good idea of the trucking industry and the potential business opportunity it offers. You also know the positives and the challenges that are common in the industry. If you're after freedom and flexibility, and can ride some short-term challenges like stress, then the trucking business is ideal for you. So, read on to find out what, specifically, you need to know about the trucking business before you start.

Chapter 2
What to Know Before You Start

Business is like war. It requires thorough preparation and strategy before getting into it. Going in blind can obliterate your business in no time. Hence, this chapter details the costs associated with starting a trucking business and how to determine the profitability of your enterprise. Most importantly, this chapter includes a plan that you can use as a roadmap so that you can begin your trucking company on the right footing and increase your chances of survival.

What to Expect When Running a Trucking Business

There is no secret that owning and running a trucking business successfully is hard work. You'll likely spend a big chunk of your time (if you are an owner-operator) hauling for your customers. Add to this the other duties small business operators have to perform, such as finding customers and building relationships, and you have a demanding task ahead of you. All these tasks require your time. This means that you may have to spend more time away from home, especially in the beginning, while putting the various business systems together.

Safety Rules and Regulations

Compliance with safety rules and regulations is essential in the trucking industry. There are plenty of these rules and regulations, which I'll talk about in more detail later in the book. Some of them include the following:

- Canadian Safety Association (CSA) safety standards (where applicable).
- The allowable hours of work for your drivers.
- Physical qualifications for truck drivers.
- Electronic logging devices for each driver to figure out the weekly hours they have worked.

Don't think of these regulations as a way to punish you. In fact, they may even dissuade others from joining the industry and thus improve your prospects of succeeding.

Costs of Starting and Owning a Trucking Company

The question of the amount of money you need to start a trucking company provides different views and answers. This is because start-up costs depend on several factors, such as the state that you're in, the size of your fleet, whether you already own a truck and have insurance, and whether you'll haul freight interstate, intrastate, or both.

Typically, a small trucking company costs about $25,000 to $40,000 to get started. This figure excludes the costs of purchasing equipment. Here are the major expenses you'll pay during the truck business start-up phase:

- Insurance down payment of between $2,000 and $4,800 a truck annually.
- The price of a truck. Which varies from $15,000 to $175,000 depending on its condition, type, and age or if you choose to buy one outright.
- State-specific tax of about $500 a truck.
- International Registration Plan (IRP) costs between $500 and $3,000.
- Business registration costs from $50 to $300, depending on your state.
- USDOT (Motor Carrier) number costs from $300 to $499.
- The International Fuel Tax Agreement (IFTA) report costs around $150.
- Unified Carrier Registration (UCR) of $69 and above.
- Trucking insurance ranging from $9,000 to $12,000 a truck annually.
- Appointing a Blanket of Coverage (BOC-3) processing agent costs from $10 to $50.

Adding up all the expenses listed above means that you'll need to set aside from $28,000 to $200,000. Note that this is an estimate. You still need to work out the exact amounts of each expense necessary to start your company. In addition, you need to factor in other expenses, such as meals, salaries, bookkeeping, parking, and tolls.

Why You Should Start With One Truck

Nothing beats growing a business organically. What do I mean by this? You see, you can choose to buy six trucks at the start of your business. If you start such a trucking business from scratch with no knowledge, skills, and experience, then the mistakes you're bound to make can wipe out the company in no time. This happens because you would have tried to jump the growth steps necessary to build the right competencies. And without the required fundamental skills, the chances of succeeding diminish greatly.

It is like these people who win the lottery and wind up broke within a few years. The lottery windfall finds them with no money management skills and all the bad habits of living. Most of them, inevitably, focus on consumption and soon use up all the money. They, essentially, return to the level where they were before winning the lottery. Money, like all tools, is an accelerator. And you can only safely accelerate something that's built on a sound foundation.

Starting with one truck provides ample opportunities to learn safely while making money. Here are some advantages of this approach:

- You reduce the amount of start-up capital to a manageable level. This minimizes the stress of looking for funding, which is better for you and your family.

- You minimize the risk of business loss. One truck means less complexity. And the simpler the business, the easier it is to run and to correct mistakes quickly. Big companies do not have the ability to respond swiftly when changes need to be made. But you will if you're operating with a single truck.

- Provides the opportunity to learn from your mistakes without putting the business at too much risk.

- Most importantly, you give yourself the time to build systems to run your business more efficiently in the future. Think about this for a moment. Would it be easier to build a safety system for one truck or for a fleet of ten? Of course, it would be easier to do so if you run one truck. And when you add a second truck, all you do is duplicate what you would have already done. This means that you'll grow your business quicker as time progresses.

The systems to consider building while operating one truck include human resources, information technology, marketing, sales, operations, technology, and so on. The power of a system is that it frees resources and enables you to do more with less. For example, with a system you can onboard a new driver much faster than another business and make fewer mistakes. Furthermore, systems allow you to deliver consistent performance, which is key to building a reputation that is so necessary in the trucking industry.

What Profits Can I Make in a Trucking Business

The profitability of your trucking business, like in any business, depends largely on how well you run your company. Well-planned trucking businesses that manage cash flow and avoid deadhead miles average around 7% of gross income per year in profit. This means that, for a company generating $300,000 of annual revenue per truck, it will profit $21,000 from every truck.

The timing of getting paid after doing the work affects your business profitability. Late payments may push you to begin shortcutting important work like truck maintenance or borrow a lot more. If you don't do maintenance in time, your trucks may often break down and cost you more in repairs. The repair costs will eat away at your profits. Borrowing money isn't free. It costs money and can pull your business back instead of strengthening it.

Furthermore, as a start-up, keep in mind that it may take several months before your company turns a sizable profit. This reason, and the one above, provide convincing evidence why having three to six months of emergency cash is so vital for your business. It will help you weather the storm in the event that you meet unforeseen events and circumstances.

You're probably wondering how much money you'll personally make when running your own trucking company. Well, this depends on your skills, experience, and competency. If you are good at getting customers and delivering what you promise, you'll make more money than the average small carrier. Trucking business owners with more experience can make around $100,000 or more, while the less experienced earn about $35,000 per year. Most owners make a healthy $50,000 annually (CDL.com, n.d.).

Do keep in mind that you'll need to provide your own truck, buy truck insurance, maintenance, and fuel. So, you do a lot more work than a driver working for a large carrier. However, your focus is not just to make money but to build an asset that will deliver cash flow even when you're no longer actively working. This can only happen if you build effective systems to run your business.

How to Estimate the Revenue of Your Trucking Company

It is important before you start your trucking company to know what revenue to expect. You're fortunate because the way to figure out your potential revenue is already available. And I'll show you here how to do it painlessly. There is no standard revenue per mile available in the industry. So, you have to figure out your own numbers. Here's how to do it.

1. **Select the Industry to Support**

   Your first task is to choose the industry in which you want to operate. This is important, as you'll see below when choosing a freight lane. More importantly, doing this enables you to buy the right truck. Imagine buying a reefer and choosing projects that require a flatbed. That would be catastrophic, isn't it?

So, choosing the industry precedes the purchasing of equipment. For example, if you choose to serve the fresh produce industry, you'll need to buy a reefer. Furthermore, selecting the industry helps you to learn the specifics like seasonality and price variations. This, in turn, allows you to plan your business much better than without this knowledge and information.

2. **Choose Freight Lane to Work**

A freight lane, also called a carrier lane or shipping lane, is a route that you routinely run to deliver truckloads. It runs from point A to point B. For example, it could run from New York to Los Angeles.

Now, it's vital to select a shipping lane that services your chosen industry and is closer to where you live. The latter is vital because you'll be able to maximize the time you spend at home. There are truck drivers that barely see their homes for days or weeks. And this may not be optimal for building healthy family relationships.

Ensure that you select carrier lanes that are near transportation "hot markets." Why is this important? Because it is easier to find loads where the demand is high. Markets like Chicago, Atlanta, Memphis, Texas, Louisiana, Seattle, and California are busy trucking companies.

3. **Figure Out the Pay-Per-Mile on Your Carrier Lane**

The following six steps will not only show you how to determine pay-per-mile on your carrier lane, but will also reveal the profitability of your shipping lane. Let's go over the six steps.

- The first thing to do is to go to a free trucking load board and look for freight in your shipping lane. A load board is nothing but an online system that lets shippers and freight brokers broadcast their freight loads.
- Second, get prices per mile on a minimum of 10 truck loads. The more, the better because the accuracy of your figures will improve.
- Thirdly, add the prices of each of the 10 loads and their corresponding miles. Now divide the total of the prices by the total number of miles. The number you have computed is the average price of each load per mile of the lane.

  Alternatively, compute each load's pay-per-mile by dividing the price by the total number of miles of each load. Then, add all the pay-per-mile numbers and divide the final answer by 10. That gives you the average price per mile of your selected freight lane in one direction.

Now you want to know the average price per mile of the same reverse lane. It's easy to do this. Simply repeat what you did above but in the reverse lane. You may find that the two prices differ. It's not uncommon for this to happen because of the role of supply and demand.

4. **Determine the Estimated Shipper Price**

This step is vital because at some point, you'd like to work directly with shippers instead of brokers. That way you can command higher prices per mile and make more revenue and profits. You see, freight brokers advertise their loads on freight boards without the markups (money added on top of the price of an item to make a profit). It's not uncommon for these brokers to add 15%, 20%, or more for their services onto the freight price you see on load boards. The price you see on the load board is what they pay you while they keep the markup.

When you know what shippers are willing to pay, you could quote competitively and thus obtain more profit. To find what shippers are comfortable paying per load per mile, let's consider an example.

Suppose a broker's cost on your freight lane is $2.70 per mile and their markup is 20%. To obtain the shipper price, all you do is divide $2.70 by 80% (that is, 100% minus 20%). And you obtain $3.38 per mile. This figure is what the shipper pays the broker. And the broker will pay $2.70 from this figure and keep a profit of $0.68 per mile.

Now that you know what the shippers pay, you can begin to market your business directly to shippers. Doing this quickly increases your pay per load and improves your profitability.

5. **Figure Out the Monthly Profitability of Your Shipping Lane**

One of the key reasons for going into business for yourself is to make as much profit as you can. So, let's work out how much monthly profit you could make on your carrier lane.

First, add the earnings per load to a destination to the amount in the return trip. This is the total income for one round-trip. By the way, a round-trip is the distance covered from a point to a destination and back to the same point. Now, multiply the total income by the number of round-trips you can reasonably complete in a month. The outcome is your monthly revenue.

Next, work out your total monthly expenses. This includes costs for fuel, parking, meals, tolls, maintenance, salaries, and so on. Subtract the expenses from the total monthly income to get your profit. Assess the number to determine if it's the kind of profit that you're comfortable with. If not, you may have to tweak either the revenue side or the expenses side to get the profit you want. We'll discuss managing finances later in the book.

Four Types of Trucking Businesses You Can Start and Run

The carrier industry consists of several types of businesses. The most common include for-hire truckload carriers, full truckload (FTL), less-than-truckload (LTL), and couriers. Which of these you want to run depends on your needs, skills, and knowledge. Let me take through each one of them in detail for you to make an informed decision.

1. **For-Hire Truckload Carriers**

   The for-hire truckload businesses haul freight belonging to other companies for money. These businesses do not manufacture or produce anything. What they do is offer a freight loading capacity to businesses that require logistic support. In essence, they hire out trucks, trailers, semi-trailers, and drivers.

   The success of these carriers depends on the shipping demands of producers and manufacturers. Such a carrier requires savvy marketing and sales skills to outbid competitors and obtain freight contracts to win business. Your business could win a shipping contract for a given period, but there's no guarantee of keeping the contract when it's due for renewal. However, the good thing is that you can hedge the loss of contracts by having multiple customers.

2. **Full Truckload (FTL)**

As the name suggests, full truckload carriers run fleets of trucks that carry dedicated shipments for their customers. The main advantage is that a truck reaches its destination quicker because it goes directly from the loading point to the delivery location. There are no pickups or drop-offs along the way to the destination.

Shippers like the fact that there is less handling of goods as this lowers the chances of loss or damage. Full truckloads are less restricted by size and weight.

3. **Less-Than-Truckload (LTL)**

Less-than-truckload companies carry multiple shipments at the same time. However, the goods are often taken to different destinations. These kinds of companies operate similarly to carpooling.

Less-than truckloads work well for smaller shipments and are often cheaper than FTL for the shippers. A customer pays according to the weight of their shipment. To optimize the available space, it's better to load one to six pallets.

Unlike FTL, LTL could result in loss or damage to goods because of multiple handling along the way. This isn't a good thing for shippers. But, as a trucker, you can ensure the shipper's goods to encourage them to do business with you.

4. **Couriers**

Couriers are door-to-door companies that often deliver goods the same day to most places. Their major competition is the standard mail delivery. The dominating benefit of couriers over standard mail delivery is that they tend to deliver quicker.

The driver personally collects and delivers the item to the receiver. Because of the personal touch involved, couriers reduce the chances of loss or damage to goods. It's possible to provide a dedicated courier truck or van to your customer to give a customized service. This helps to strengthen your business relationship with shippers.

Those are the four major trucking business options that you have and can select from. Irrespective of the trucking option you choose, you still need to decide whether you'll hire drivers or become an owner-operator. And the choice you make will dictate how you operate your business.

The final decision depends mainly on the more cost-effective approach. Most importantly, your business skills will help you decide the better route to follow. If you desire to drive a truck, perhaps becoming an owner-operator is the right route for you. However, you should know that it is hard work.

Prepare and Craft a Business Plan

Lack of planning is one of the factors responsible for business failure. Creating a business plan is a trusted way of alleviating this problem. What is a business plan? It's simply a roadmap that has a clear target that shows where you're taking your company and how you'll do it. Contrary to what some people think, a business plan doesn't have to be a 500-page document detailing every action you will take while building your business in the next 10 or 20 years.

A business plan offers a blueprint that guides you towards attaining your business goal(s). When written thoughtfully, a business plan serves several purposes. Firstly, it helps you to apply and successfully get business funding for your trucking company. This is the money that you can use to buy additional trucks if you want to expand. Secondly, a business plan shows how you're going to sell your products and services and thus generates cash flow, the lifeblood of any company.

Your business plan should include the following sections:

- **The executive summary**: This provides a short overview of your trucking company and plans to achieve your business goal(s). It's a good idea to write it last, after completing the other parts.

- **Company description**: Here you provide the business background. It's vital to include what sets your trucking company apart from its competitors. Without uniqueness, your business will just look like the rest and fail to attract your target customers' attention. Furthermore, provide details of who owns and manages the business as well as the roles and responsibilities of the employees (if applicable).

- **Services**: This section delivers an outline of the services that you'll offer to your target market. It also tells how you plan to meet customer and market demand. It's a good idea to reveal your pricing structure, the goods you plan to load and the industries you'll support.

- **Market Analysis**: This section is the heart of your business plan. It provides data that proves that there is a market for your business. It shows how you plan to win new business and beat your competitors. Some components to include here are:
    - Description of the trucking industry and its outlook.
    - Who is your target market and where you'll find them.
    - Pricing and the profit margin.
    - Competitor analysis. This means telling the weaknesses and strengths of your rivals to show how you discovered a competitive advantage.
    - The regulatory environment and how it can impact your business. Importantly, you need to show how you'll handle regulatory challenges.

- **Sales and Marketing**: Together with market analysis, the sales and marketing sections make up a considerable chunk of your business plan's value. This section focuses on providing strategies to find prospective customers. It doesn't help much to only find customers, you still must generate cash from them. Divide this section into two subsections like this:

- ○ **Marketing strategy**: This subsection details exactly what you'll do to get clients and grow your base of customers. Mention the means you'll use to market your company, such as direct mail, networking, online marketing, and social media. It's vital to include an estimate of your marketing budget to meet your identified objectives.

- ○ **Sales Strategy**: Here you need to explain how you'll turn prospects into customers who buy. Spell out how you'll sell your services. Are you going to hire sales agents or a third party? Think through your selling strategies carefully because there's no cash flow without sales and, therefore, no business.

- **Funding request**: If you're producing the business plan for funding purposes, this is the section to spell that out clearly. You need to be clear about the amount of money you request and its purpose. Most importantly, include what you'll give in return for the funds, such as equity. Don't overlook spelling out the terms of your offer, such as the exit strategy both for you and your funder(s).

- **Financial projections**: The financial projections will depend on the trucking industry's outlook and your market share. The numbers that you include here should cover the break-even analysis. Most importantly, include in your projections your balance sheet, profit and loss statement, cash flow statement, and the sales forecast.

Those are all the key sections to include in your plan. Even if you're not going to seek funding, it helps to go through the business planning process. The reason you do this is to ensure you think through all aspects of your trucking business. That way, you'll improve your chances of survival.

Eight Must-Know Reasons Why Trucking Businesses Fail

I've just gone through the business planning process with you to avoid starting a carrier with minimal chances of survival. I did that because 85% of trucking companies fail in their first year of operations. This means that a mere 15% see the second year (CDL.com, n.d.). Isn't it essential to know why there is such a high failure rate of trucking companies? It is vital to know and I'll share with you the eight reasons why these businesses fold so quickly.

1. **Inadequate Business Planning**

   A plan tells you where you are and where you're going. Unfortunately, owners of some trucking businesses fail to craft thoughtful business plans. And as a consequence, their companies fail to survive, some not even the first year. It is for his reason why I included the previous section in this book.

   The trucking industry has many regulations plus a unique target market. You need to think through these aspects of a trucking business to understand the industry and plan how you'll reach your goals. For example, your plan should be clear about how you'll handle these regulations and future changes. Furthermore, you need to think about how you'll build relationships with your target market.

   Most importantly, it's vital to review your plan at regular intervals, such as quarterly or half-yearly, to ensure you're still on track. Or to adjust the plan, if need be.

2. **Poor Business Management**

   I've always found it difficult to manage anything that I don't measure. To manage means to ensure something does what it is supposed to do. This means that you first need to define what your business should do. And this is where your business plan comes in and provides the business measures to work towards.

When you begin running your business, it's vital to keep numbers such as sales, number of customers, miles you're covering, the freight lanes you're working, and so on. Then you'd be able to determine whether you are running your business according to the plan you would have crafted or not.

There are two major groups of numbers to keep. The financial numbers which you can record and keep yourself or for which you could hire a bookkeeper. These numbers tell you quickly where the money is coming from, how much of it there is, and where it goes. The second group of numbers comes from your operations. They are operations numbers that indicate how efficient you're running your business. Such numbers include the number of round-trips you complete per week, month, and year.

Keeping numbers is a big part of running any successful business. Without keeping a scorecard in a basketball match, how do you know who won? So it is in the trucking business. So, ensure you keep the right numbers.

3. **Inadequate Cash Flow**

When a trucking business doesn't bring in money, often owners say that they have a cash flow problem. Yet, a careful look into the business will reveal that the problem isn't cash flow. If cash flow were the problem, solutions would focus on it. But a short time in business will reveal to you that cash flow is a result of business activities like sales and cost control.

So, inadequate cash flow is the outcome of a business operation that's gone wrong. Some of those issues include the following:

- Not getting enough customers.
- Having several outstanding invoices.
- High cost of operations such as excessive truck breakdowns and truck fuel inefficiency.

To solve these problems, you should first analyze your business numbers to locate those responsible for low cash flow. Then figure out ways to solve them one at a time. For quick cash flow improvement, I suggest solving the high-impact issue first.

4. **No or Ineffective Collection Strategy**

Your customers are unlikely to pay you cash for your trucking services. They may commit to paying you in 30, 45, or 60 days after invoicing them. Still, when the invoice is due, they may not be able to pay.

That's where your collection system kicks in. This system will help you to identify unpaid accounts well in time and act swiftly. With an effective collection strategy, you'll notice fewer cash flow issues due to unpaid invoices. I'll provide details in Chapter 6 on what to include in your collection strategy.

5. **Lack of Knowledge of Market Rates**

We covered market rates of freight lanes earlier in the book. At this point, you should be familiar with how to determine your carrier lane's pay-per-mile. This enables you to quote your customers correctly. If you're underquoting for some weird reason, nothing prevents you from adjusting your rates in future loads.

Without adjusting, your rates could land your business in negative profit territory. And no business can survive for long with no profit. This is because such a business will need a cash injection from elsewhere to close the cash flow gaps. And that's not a positive sign of a profitable business.

6. **Non-Compliance to Legal and Safety Regulations**

I'm sure by now you're noticing that most of the factors that result in trucking business failures are related to business planning. If you recall, one of the items to think through during business planning is the regulatory environment. Unfortunately, some trucking businesses overlook doing this work upfront. And soon enough, their misstep catches up with them. I don't want you to be a victim of this oversight.

Also, regulations often change. Are you geared to catch them and adjust your business when this happens? You should. This means that you need to have ways to keep track of applicable regulatory changes. Failure to catch and comply with regulations could result in fines and possible shutdown by the Department of Transportation (DOT). Furthermore, complying with regulations minimizes headaches and stress, and helps you to run your carrier profitably.

One of the powerful things to do is to write a detailed safety plan. Then, you need to keep training and refreshing your drivers so that they stay informed and competent to comply with transportation law.

7. **Forming Partnerships With the Wrong People**

Business partnerships can be great. Partners share work and contribute resources like capital. The load of running a trucking business becomes lighter. But things can go wrong. One or more of the partners may begin to abdicate their responsibility. And this could create tensions and possible business failure.

Entering into a legal partnership agreement that spells out each partner's responsibility provides some protection. It's vital to ensure that you include an exit strategy in the agreement that protects both partners. In fact, any contract or agreement that you enter into should have an exit strategy to protect you from possible financial ruin.

8. The Owners Fail to Seek Professional Help

A trucking business has several aspects that need to be taken care of. Some activities that need regular attention include accounting, safety management, vehicle maintenance, marketing, law, and sales. Sometimes (and it often happens), it can be hard to cover all of them because you have a limited amount of time, energy, and mental power. You don't have to let your business suffer because of this.

There are professionals, like bookkeepers, lawyers, safety managers, and so on, who can help reduce your workload. Not only will you free up some of your time and energy, but you'll also think clearer and run your business better. However, keep in mind that delegation doesn't mean you're not responsible. You still need to ensure those who help you do the right work because the buck stops with you in your business.

You're now in a position to begin learning how to get started with your trucking company.

Chapter 3
Getting Started

This chapter will take you through the steps to take to get started, from business registration to applying for business insurance. I cover all the documentation and licenses you need for you to get started right in your trucking business journey.

This information is vital because it helps you get started the right way. Let's get started right away.

Business Registration

There are four common types of business for the small business operator. You must understand each of them to select the kind that meets your needs. You have a choice of either a sole proprietorship, partnership, limited liability company, or corporation. The choice you make brings with it certain legal and financial implications. One significant implication is the taxes you'll need to pay to keep your business on a legal footing. Let's go over each of these kinds of business entities so you can make an intelligent choice.

1. **Sole Proprietorship**

   A sole proprietor is the simplest type of business entity. It's ideal for a person who owns and runs the business by themselves. By law, immediately when you start a new business as a sole owner you become a sole proprietor.

There's no need to register with the state as a sole proprietor. However, note that you might need to apply for certain licenses or permits carrying out your business. This depends on the kind of industry in which your company operates.

- **The good of a sole proprietor**
  - It is easy to file for tax when running a sole proprietor.
  - You're allowed to deduct allowable business deductions and business losses when filing your tax returns.
  - There's no need to fill in complex documentation such as meetings.
  - You don't need to register this kind of business with the state.
- **The other side of a sole proprietor**
  - You're personally liable for debts and liabilities of your business. This is the one reason why some people avoid sole proprietors when starting businesses.
  - It's tougher to access funding, such as business loans and raising money from investors.
  - Building business credit isn't easy.

2. **Limited Liability Company (LLC)**

A limited liability company protects you from personal liability in the event of lawsuits, debts, and liabilities. The reason is that your business operates separately from the business owner. It is like a separate individual with their own assets and liabilities. A potential plaintiff cannot sue you for your business liabilities. They sue your LLC directly. It requires less paperwork compared to corporations.

Your LLC can be taxed either as a sole proprietor or a corporation depending on your choice. It's possible to add more members to an LLC. However, it is slightly more pricey to create an LLC instead of a partnership or sole proprietorship. This is mainly because you must register the LLC with the state.

- **How to Set Up an LLC**

    The requirements for setting up an LLC vary from one state to the next. The good thing is that the setting up process takes only from one to four hours. Here's what you need to do to register your LLC.

    ○ **Make a Copy of Your State's LLC Articles of Organization Form**

    The Articles of Organization Form is obtainable online from your Secretary of State's website or at their offices. Find out from the Secretary's office if it's necessary to post a notice in the newspaper and their rules regarding business names.

o **Fill Out the Articles of Organization Form**

The Articles of Organization Form is simple to fill, and you can do it by yourself. All that's required are things like the name of your business, principal office address, registered agent, and the names of members of the LLC.

o **Post a Notice in Your Local Newspaper**

You can only post a notice in your local newspaper if it's a requirement in your state. If it's not required, then skip this step.

o **Send Your Articles of Organization Form to Your Secretary of State**

When you have filled in your Articles of Organization form, you are ready to send it to your Secretary of State. This stage requires a filing fee that ranges from $40 to $900 and varies by state (Scott, 2018).

Some states like California charge a corporate tax that you need to pay when you set up your LLC. This fee is separate from the filing fee. So, in some states registering an LLC could be a bit expensive compared to others. Here are the costs of filing an LLC per state (Akalp, 2015):

State	Cost of filing an LLC
Alabama	$165
Alaska	$250
Arizona	$50
Arkansas	$50
California	$75
Colorado	$50
Connecticut	$175
District of Columbia	$220
Delaware	$140
Florida	$155
Georgia	$100

Hawaii	$50

State	Cost of filing an LLC
Idaho	$100
Illinois	$500
Indiana	$90
Iowa	$50
Kansas	$160
Kentucky	$55
Louisiana	$100
Maine	$175
Maryland	$155
Massachusetts	$520
Michigan	$50
Minnesota	$160

Mississippi	$50
Missouri	$50
Montana	$70
Nebraska	$120
Nevada	$75
New Hampshire	$100
New Jersey	$125
New Mexico	$50
New York	$210
North Carolina	$125

State	Cost of filing an LLC
North Dakota	$135
Ohio	$125
Oklahoma	$104

Oregon	$100
Pennsylvania	$125
Rhode Island	$125
South Carolina	$110
South Dakota	$150
Tennessee	$325
Texas	$310
Utah	$72
Vermont	$125
Virginia	$104
Washington	$200
West Virginia	$132
Wisconsin	$103
Wyoming	$103

Now you know what filing fees to expect in each of the states you want to operate your trucking business.

Does Your Business Operate Under a Different Name?

Some businesses operate using names that are different from their official names. This is legal. If you plan to do this, you should file a D/B/A (Trade Name or "Fictitious" Name) with your county.

Some states require you to file your business with them. It's a good idea to check with your state to avoid trouble later on.

Licenses and Permits You Need

Your trucking business must comply with all the necessary licensing and regulations before starting to operate. Failure may result in the loss of your business and subsequent forfeiture of any money you used. There are several licenses and permits you need, including a Commercial Driver's License (CDL), operating authority, and International Fuel Tax Agreement (IFTA). Let's discuss each of these permits and licenses and how to obtain them.

A Commercial Driver's License (CDL)

A CDL is a permission to drive large, heavy trucks or vehicles carrying hazardous substances on public roads in the U.S. If you already drive for another trucking company, there's no need to read this section of the book because you already have this license.

To obtain this license, you need to nail a knowledge and skills test. Failure to pass this test may result in your CDL having unwanted restrictions. Here are the steps to follow to obtain a CDL.

- Ensure that you are 21 years or older before you apply for a CDL. If you only want to drive intrastate, you must be at least 18 years old. I advise you to check with your state for the exact age restrictions that might be in place.

- Obtain and study your state's CDL manual. This document, also called the CDL Handbook, contains the content you need to study to pass a written CDL test. You'll also find vehicle classifications and age restrictions in some states' CDL manuals. It's easy to get your copy of this manual. Head over to the internet and type in "[Your state's name] CDL manual pdf" and you'll be directed to the right place.

- Select the type of truck or vehicle and the kind of driving you want to do. CDLs cover three classes of vehicles and each of these requires specific endorsements and requirements.

- Fill and hand in your state's CDL application and pay the applicable fees. Again, the internet makes it easy to obtain this form online.

- Supply proof of identity, residency, and social security number. You may use your social security card or Medicare ID card as evidence of your social security number. As for your identity, documents like your U.S. birth certificate and U.S. passport are acceptable. To prove residency, simply submit a recent copy of a utility bill. I suggest that you check with your state the actual acceptable documents to confirm your identity, residence, and social security number.

- Provide medical proof of fitness. To obtain a CDL, you'll be required to prove that you're medically fit to drive large commercial vehicles. You do this by supplying the Medical Examination Report Form (MCSA-5875) and the Medical Examiner's Certificate Form (MCSA-5876). Further legibility may involve checking your driving record over the previous 10 years in all states.

- Take and pay for the vision test and knowledge exam. Once you're successful with these tests, you obtain your Commercial Learner's Permit(CLP). This permit authorizes you to drive a commercial vehicle on public roads under the supervision of a qualified CDL holder.

- Obtain the CDL. After obtaining the CLP, you should wait for 14 days before you take the CDL skills test. Some states require you to complete CDL training first successfully.

There are three tests that you should pass to get your CDL, namely:

- o The vehicle inspection test.
- o The basic control test.
- o The road test.

The easiest way to nail all the above tests is to practice each of them using the CDL manual. Because you have the CLP at this stage, I suggest that you get access to a truck and physically practice the tests on a real vehicle. Getting a coach to help you simulate the actual CDL test conditions can help you eliminate nervousness when taking the exams.

On successfully completing your CDL tests submit the filled documents for processing. You could obtain your CDL the same day or it may be delivered to you through the mail.

USDOT Number

To reiterate, a USDOT Number uniquely identifies your carrier during events like crash investigations and audits. Transporting freight in interstate commerce requires a company to register with the FMCSA and carry a USDOT Number. The USDOT Number is also required for the hauling of intrastate hazardous materials that require a safety permit. Some states require a trucking company to have a DOT Number.

One of the easiest ways to determine if you need to have a USDOT number is using an FMCSA **tool**. It will take you through a series of few questions. Once you have answered all the questions, you'll know whether you need this vital permit or not. If you find that you do need the USDOT Number, then it's time to apply for one. The FMCSA requires all new USDOT Number applicants to use the online Unified Registration System (URS) to obtain the permit. This mode of application debuted on December 12, 2015 and simplified registrations for various permits.

It takes about four to six weeks to get your USDOT Number. Upon obtaining this permit, display it on both sides of your trucks. Doors often provide an ideal location to stick the USDOT Number. Importantly, a person must be able to clearly see and read the USDOT Number from up to 50 feet away.

The USDOT Number opens the way for you to apply for the trucking authority explained below.

Trucking (Operating) Authority

A trucking authority provides evidence that the government gave your company permission to receive payment for moving freight. Instead of calling it the trucking authority, some people refer to it as the Motor Carrier (MC) number. You obtain the permit from the Federal Motor Carrier Safety Administration (FMCSA).

There are multiple authorities depending on the kind of work that you do in the freight industry. You may need to obtain the motor carrier authority, broker authority, freight forwarder authority, or both. Only apply for the authority relevant to the jobs you perform to save yourself time and money. Whatever authority you have determines the required financial responsibility to keep, such as the level of insurance you.

Unified Carrier Registration (UCR)

The Unified Carrier Registration (UCR) Plan and Agreement authorizes states to collect fees from qualifying trucking companies and brokers. These fees serve for tasks like USDOT officer training and to support state safety programs. However, not all states participate in the UCR Plan and Agreement. So, if you're only hauling goods intrastate, check with the state if they require UCR registration or not. A UCR offers officers a way to check and verify if you have active insurance coverage in states where you do business.

The application fee for UCR depends on the fleet size that qualifies to be included. Some companies may operate a fleet interstate, including in states not part of the UCR Plan and Agreement. In that case, not all the fleet may qualify for UCR registration. Registration opens on October 1 and runs through to December 31. Failure to pay UCR fees could result in fines and penalties. And so, you may wind up affecting the cash flow and profitability of your business by failing to abide by this regulation.

To apply for the UCR, simply head over to their website. You'll be asked to enter your USDOT Number and MC Number to proceed.

Heavy Vehicle Use Tax (HVUT)

The Heavy Vehicle Use Tax (HVUT) is an annual fee charged on heavy vehicles that run on public highways and weigh 55,000 pounds or more. The gross weight quoted includes the following:

- The weight of an unloaded vehicle ready to do its work.
- The weight of an unloaded trailer or semi trailer ready for service and its often used.
- The weight of the maximum freight carried by the vehicle and trailer or semitrailer combination.

The above weight determines the fees you'll to pay in the following manner (DOT Federal Highway Administration, 2020):

- For gross weight lying between 55,000 and 75,000 pounds, the fee is $100 plus $22 for every 1,000 pounds above the 55,000 pounds.
- If your vehicle weighs over 75,000, the HVUT is $550.

The HVUT is payable using Form 2290 available from the Internal Revenue Service (IRS). You don't have to file this form separately. The easiest way is to file it at the same time with your tax returns.

International Fuel Tax Agreement (IFTA)

The International Fuel Tax Agreement (IFTA) license permits you to pay fuel taxes to multiple member jurisdictions at a go. This means that you don't have to file the tax for each state separately. So, the process simplifies fuel tax payments for interstate and commercial trucking companies. Therefore, it's prudent to register your trucking company if you run interstate freight.

Not every truck qualifies to be included for IFTA purposes. The vehicle must be registered if it meets either of the following criteria (Boyers, 2020):

- The vehicle must have two axles and a gross weight of 26,000 and above.
- Any weight and has three axles or more.
- A vehicle used in combination and weighs over 26,000 pounds.

It is easy to apply for an IFTA license. Head over to your state's website and apply there. Note that the application forms may differ from one state to the next. On being successful with your application, you'll receive IFTA decals that expire on December 31 annually. The regulation gives you until March 1 of the subsequent year before you must carry new decals.

Standard Carrier Alpha Code (SCAC)

The Standard Carrier Alpha Code (SCAC) is a two- to four-letter code used to identify transportation companies. It helps the government to regulate transport services for tasks like border control and sticking to environmental standards. Most importantly, a trucking company doing business with many shippers must have it.

It's easy to get this code. All you do is head over to the National Motor Freight Traffic Association's website and apply or renew your SCAC code. The application fee to obtain the SCAC is $70 (STANDARD

CARRIER ALPHA CODE (SCAC) APPLICATION, n.d.).

Blanket of Coverage (BOC-3) Permit

The blanket of coverage (BOC-3) permit authorizes the legal presence of trucking companies, freight brokers, and freight forwarders. Filling the BOC-3 Form is a way to designate process agents who represent your freight company in each state where you haul goods.

For example, if there is a legal issue against your trucking business, the process agent will accept court papers on your behalf. You're not allowed to fill the BOC-3 form by yourself. This is a task only process agents do. Your role in this is to select the process agent to complete the form for you.

It costs between $20 and $40 to get the form filled out and processed. For ease of administration, it's way better to choose a process agent who operates in all the states where you do business.

Often, business people desiring to enter the trucking industry find the processes lengthy and cumbersome. There's a way around this obstacle. Companies such as GLAuthority can help you apply for all the necessary permits for a modest fee. I advise new truck owners to understand still what's involved even if they hire such a company. If something goes wrong, you'll understand and solve it much faster than someone who doesn't.

Comply with Local Laws and Apply for Applicable laws

Rules and laws vary from state to state. Some rules are common such as the requirement to apply for a health permit if handling food products.

Register for Different Taxes

Each trucking should register for several taxes, including income tax, sales tax, and self-employment tax. You must register for all applicable taxes to keep your business away from troubles. You may have to pay taxes at federal, state, and local levels. The amount of tax you pay depends on the kinds of business activities your company does.

Let's go over the process of registering for these taxes.

1. **Obtain Employer Identification Number (EIN)**

   The Employer Identification Number is also called Federal Tax Identification Number. It is a unique nine-digit number used to identify a business for tax reasons. Having the EIN enables you to get things like business accounts and licenses. You can apply for the EIN online. The IRS asks you a series of simple questions and you provide the answers. This is the easiest and fastest way of getting the EIN.

   You need to have the following when applying for the EIN: The name and Taxpayer Identification Number of the business owner, principal officer, or general partner. This person must be the one who manages or directs the assets of the business. A business entity cannot be used for this purpose.

2. **Register for State Tax**

   Any company that does business in a state has what's called tax presence. This means that the business must pay state income, sales excise, and state employment taxes provided it has employees.

The first step of the process is to register with the state's revenue department for income tax. However, some states like Washington, South Dakota, and Florida don't have an income tax. So, make sure your base state requires you to pay income tax.

A business that sells products and services that attract sales tax must apply for a tax seller's permit in the state they operate. The sales tax is also called a trust fund tax. This permit allows you to collect, report, and pay the sales tax to the state. Most states have an online presence for easy registration. Not all states charge sales tax, such as Alaska, Delaware, and Montana.

If you have a tax presence in a state and hire employees, you need to register with your state's employment bureau by law. This allows you to collect income taxes from employees on behalf of the state. Furthermore, you should pay state unemployment taxes and the worker's compensation fund.

Important: If you do business in multiple states, you must register with each state for tax purposes. In the state you first register with your business is deemed a domestic entity. And in the remainder of the states you register as a foreign business entity.

3. **Income Tax**

All businesses must pay income tax based on the amount of profit they make. The form of the business dictates how you'll pay this tax. For example, a sole proprietor requires that you add net income from Schedule C and your income from other sources to determine your total tax. On the other hand, LLC owners can choose to pay tax like a sole proprietor or as a corporation. And thus, an LLC owner paying tax as a sole proprietor will pay a different tax amount than in a corporation having equal revenues.

As a business owner, the law allows you to deduct certain expenses before reporting your taxable income. The regular business expenses to deduct are numerous. The key is to ensure that you deduct only costs you incurred for business purposes. Most importantly, you must have proof for each deduction that you make. Some expenses you may deduct include the following.:

- Business meals.
- Business insurance.
- Work-related travel costs.
- Advertising and promotion.
- Professional services like accounting and office cleaning.

There's also another kind of business deduction that you can make. It is called qualified business income deduction (QBI). This law came in force in the 2018 tax year and will continue until 2025. Using QBI, you're allowed to deduct up to 20 percent of qualified business income (Murray, 2020). However, the deduction applies only for business owners who pay their business taxes on their personal tax returns.

Notice that (QBI) deduction adds to the usual acceptable business expense deductions.

4. **Self-Employment Taxes**

Self-employment taxes serve to fund Social Security and Medicare. The amount you pay depends, like income tax, on the net income of the business. This means that when your business makes no profit, there won't be a self-employment tax. It doesn't stop there. Not paying self-employment taxes results in no Social Security and Medicare credits for that year. So, if you want to increase Social Security and Medicare credits every year, you must keep making profits annually.

Not every business owner pays self-employment taxes: only sole proprietors, partners making up a partnership, and LLC owners

5. **Sales Tax**

Sales tax gets paid on sales of qualifying products and services that businesses sell. The government charges a certain percentage on every sale of certain products and services. The good thing for the business owner is that this tax isn't your responsibility. It is the consumers who pay it.

The business's role is to collect this tax, report, and pay it to the government. You need to have a system to collect and account for sales tax to avoid mistaking it for your business revenue or profit.

6. **Gross Receipts Tax**

Most states require businesses to pay a state income tax, as we've discussed above. However, states like Nevada and Texas charge gross receipts (revenue) tax, either adding to state income tax or replacing it.

Not all business types are eligible for gross receipts tax. It's therefore essential to check with your state if your business is eligible for this tax. Sole proprietors often ineligible for paying gross receipts tax although they still pay state income tax.

7. **IFTA Fuel Tax Returns**

We've already discussed what IFTA fuel taxes are. Now it's time to understand how a trucking business pays for them. The crucial thing is to ensure that you have your accurate IFTA reporting documents and file the return in time to avoid fines, penalties, and energy-sapping external audits.

IFTA fuel taxes get paid quarterly. The due dates are as follows:

- April 30 for the first quarter.
- July 31 for the second quarter.
- October 31 for the third quarter.

- January 31 of the following year for the fourth quarter.

It is easy to pay for IFTA taxes. The IFTA members have streamlined the process to allow you to pay these taxes online through the Department of Revenue's IFTA Fuel Tax System. This system can help you do more than only pay taxes.

You can use it to request additional IFTA decals and manage other issues related to this regulation.

Preparing and paying IFTA fuel tax can be a life-sucking exercise. The way around this issue is to utilize IFTA reporting software. That way, you'll simplify the IFTA tax paying and reporting processes, save time, and improve efficiency. I show how to work out your IFTA fuel taxes in Chapter 6 so that you know how the software generates these taxes.

Receiving Payments from Your Customers

When you complete loads for your customers you want to get paid. So, you'll issue an invoice, and the customer will pay it within the agreed time. However, the customer will want to know the ways available to pay your invoice. There are several ways of receiving money for the services and products you offer to your customers. It's easier for your customers if you give them a variety of options. Whatever options you choose, you should ensure that they'll simplify your downstream processes like cost reviews and filing tax returns.

The key step before identifying any invoice payment options is to open a business bank account. There are good reasons for doing this.

Why You Should Open a Bank Account and Business Credit Card

Some business owners make a serious money management mistake. They combine their personal money with the business cash. This makes accounting for business income difficult. And that can make paying the relevant taxes a nightmare. So, to simplify your personal and business money management processes, it's essential to open separate bank accounts. One account for your business and another for personal use.

Usually, at this point, you already have a personal bank account. All you need to do now is to open a business bank account. It starts with shopping around for banks that offer cost-effective bank accounts. Also, consider the reputation of the bank when deciding where to open a bank account. One of the great benefits of a bank account is that it will simplify cost management and tax filing.

The other important money management tool is a business credit card. It helps you to keep your business expenses in one place for easy managing and control of credit. Furthermore, it helps your trucking business build a credit history, which can be handy when looking for funding to expand your fleet, for example.

Like with a bank account, shop around for a bank or credit union that offers good credit cards and rewards.

Now, let's talk about the right ways you may receive payments.

1. **Your Business Bank Account**

   Getting paid directly into your business account is the easiest method you can use. Because it's direct, the only costs you may pay will be bank charges. You don't have to do anything special to get paid this way. Simply include your business bank details in your invoice. If you prefer this method, let your customer know on the invoice.

2. **Point of Sale Payment**

   Three things are necessary for you to be paid through a point of sale system. You need to have a bank account, a credit card merchant account, and a payment processing device.

   It costs $50 to $200 in start-up fees and monthly transaction fees. It's not uncommon for transaction fees to be around five to 50 cents per purchase. Monthly fees often hover around $4 to $20 a month.

3. **Online Payment Systems**

   Online systems have become increasingly important, especially for businesses operating online. One big player in online payment systems is PayPal. It's easy to use PayPal because you don't need to be an expert on computers. All you need is to register a business account online. Then, they'll inform you what documentation they need, if necessary.

Once your account activates, you simply locate and choose a "Buy Now" code and paste it into your website. Your customers then click on the button to pay for your services and products. They'll be taken through a simple process until the transaction completes. Transaction fees start from 0.7% to 2.9% of the invoice value plus 30 cents per order. Your sales volume will influence the actual fees that you pay.

Business Insurance

The purpose of business insurance is to protect your business and its assets financially. The kinds of insurance you need depend on the nature of your business and circumstances. What's common on all insurance is that you should shop around for cost-effective insurance products with attractive terms.

Let's talk about the types of insurances you need as a trucking business.

1. **General Liability Insurance**

   General liability insurance protects your business against financial loss due to events like bodily harm, property damage, medical expenses, defending lawsuits, and judgments. These events are often out of your control and that's where a general liability insurance comes in.

In the freight industry, you'll need anywhere from $300,000 to $5,000,000, depending on the kinds of goods you transport (Federal Motor Carrier Safety Administration, 2019). A $1,000,000 cover finds acceptance with many shippers and freight brokers (Getloaded, n.d.).

2. **Commercial Property Insurance**

Commercial property insurance covers loss against damage to business property, such as vehicles and buildings. Property damage may occur due to events like fire, hurricanes, and other disasters beyond your control. The value of commercial property insurance you need depends on the type and condition of the assets you protect.

3. **Home-Based Business Owner's Insurance**

A home-based business owner's insurance is limited liability protection covering a small amount of equipment and third party injury. It adds to your normal homeowner's insurance.

Check with your homeowner's insurer if they accept running a business at your home. Operating a business from home may attract higher premiums and deductibles.

4. **Business Owner Insurance**

A business owner insurance serves to simplify insurance for business owners. What it does is to bundle different insurance products into a single policy. This simplifies your business life because you only have to deal with one company and one policy instead of five or six policies.

5. **Cargo Insurance**

   A cargo insurance protects your business against loss due to damage or loss of freight. A cargo insurance of $100,000 provides sufficient cover for most freight companies (Getloaded, n.d.). However, the exact amount of coverage depends on the type of cargo you load.

6. **Physical Damage Insurance**

   A physical damage insurance protects your trucking business in case your truck gets involved in an accident where someone else is at fault.

7. **Non-Trucking Use (Bobtail) Insurance**

   Non-trucking use insurance protects your business if your truck gets involved in an accident without your customer's load.

The above are the major types of insurances that you need to have in your trucking business. Where possible, try to bundle them together to minimize the amount of paperwork you need to handle. Doing so will further save you time and money.

When shopping around for insurances, ensure you do the following, amongst other things:

- Compare premiums and terms.

- Check if there's any business revenue cap for each insurance to ensure your company stays covered even when it grows.
- Ensure that you buy adequate coverage to avoid out-of-pocket expenses.
- Verify that your property and the area of business qualify for each business insurance cover.

Having registered your business and getting the required permits and licenses, you now are ready to begin building your fleet of trucks.

Chapter 4
Building Your Fleet

Starting a trucking business may seem costly and it is if you don't have the finances. Just to start, it may require in the vicinity of $20,000 to $40,000 without adding trucks. Considering that a truck can cost anywhere from $15,000 to $175,000 you're looking at a significant amount of money to start. And for a down payment, it's not uncommon to have to pay $1,000 to $10,000 depending on your vehicle choice and condition of the truck.

Despite this seemingly large amount of start-up money, you can still launch a trucking company. You don't necessarily need to have a lot of money to get started in the trucking industry. You need the right information, and this chapter shows you some funding options you have available. Before we talk about funding itself, let's discuss the kinds of trucks and costs you can expect.

Which is Better, a New or Used Truck?

Trucks are the foundation of any trucking business. Therefore, you need to have trucks that are in good condition to complete the delivery of your customers' loads. With this idea in mind, it should be easy to notice that it's not about whether the truck is new or old, but that it can do the job at hand.

However, there are advantages to buying new trucks as opposed to second-hand models. The most significant benefit of new trucks is lower maintenance. Because they're new, they'll likely give you significant mileage before beginning to have problems. But new trucks cost a lot more to purchase than second-hand types. You'll need to have at least $100,000 to buy a new truck.

On the other hand, second-hand trucks can be cost-effective, provided that their maintenance is up to date and their files are in order. Roadworthy, used trucks attract lower annual insurances, resulting in lower fixed costs for your business. This could slightly increase your profit. One example is buying a five-year-old or younger rig driven by a Detroit Diesel engine with less than 600,000 miles in it. It can still give you good, solid performance of eight to ten years but can be a bit pricey.

Although naturally you may want to save on equipment, the decision may backfire down the road. For example, you may face countless breakdowns and frequent repairs later on. This can result in higher maintenance and repair costs reducing your profits.

If you decide to buy a second-hand truck, you need to do your homework. The most important things to check for include:

- The truck's record of maintenance and history of oil changes. You want a vehicle with proof that it received maintenance in time and the right work completed each time. If you don't know how to read the maintenance record, consider finding someone competent to help you. This matter is not to be taken lightly at all.
- The condition of the tire tread.

- The mileage of the truck. The lower the mileage, the better the truck is likely to be.
- Rust on the truck's body and any other visible signs of body damage, a sign that the truck may have been involved in an accident. Such a truck is a no-go because there may be unnoticeable damage to the structure and even the truck's engine. Buying it could simply be a costly decision indeed.

There are still other important things to consider when you buy trucks.

Buy Trucks that Matches Your Business Plan

You'll recall that we spent time earlier on developing a sound business plan. This plan provided you with a chance to think about the type of customers you want to support. That immediately informs you of the type of trucks you'll need to have in your fleet. For example, to haul perishable goods, you'll need trucks equipped with refrigerated compartments to keep the items fresh.

Another factor to keep in mind is whether you'll be doing short-haul or long-haul routes. Long-haul trucks quickly rack up mileage and tend to break down more often than short-haul. So, if borrowing money, you may have to pay a more considerable amount of down payment and higher interest rates because of more risk.

Furthermore, the kind of trucks that you need for short-haul tend to differ from the long-haul vehicles. And these differences affect their prices, maintenance, and insurance.

At last, what matters is to ensure that the trucks you buy match your business plan. The reason is that you'll be able to complete your customer loads and be paid according to your expectations. And thus, you'll improve your chances of success in this tough trucking industry.

Best Makes (Brands) of Trucks

Deciding the make and model of the trucks in your fleet isn't an easy task. It doesn't matter whether you're an experienced truck driver wanting to buy a truck or you're unfamiliar with the trucking industry. It's still difficult to decide on the best make to purchase for two reasons. First, your money is involved and you don't want to make a mistake. And secondly, buying a truck is a matter of personal taste and the kinds of loads you plan to carry.

Therefore, you should take time and do thorough research, especially if you're new to the freight industry. Here are some questions to answer when choosing a brand:

- Will you be doing short-haul, long-haul, or local deliveries?
- What style of truck cab do you prefer?
- Are you buying a new or second-hand truck?
- Will you be financing, leasing, or paying in cash up front?
- Are there emission standards that the truck must meet?

Short-haul and local freight trucks don't have to have similar features as long-haul trucks. The main attribute you want in a short-haul or local truck is mechanical soundness and solid build quality. The source of the truck isn't an overly important matter. But you want to buy from a dealership that understands your business and is reputable.

On the other hand, long-haul trucks can experience breakdowns in all sorts of places. So, you want to buy the truck from a dealership with locations throughout the U.S. This ensures that you can get up and running in no time and still operate a profitable business. Brands such as Kenworth and Peterbilt have locations at strategic places throughout the country to support long-haul trucking companies.

Now, let's talk about what kind of trailers you may need for your business.

Different Types of Trailers

There are a variety of trailers that are suitable for different kinds of loading requirements. It is vital to select a trailer that will do the job efficiently.

1. **Dry Van**

    A dry van is a semitrailer with a long enclosed rectangular box sitting on wheels. It protects the freight from the weather and other things that could affect the quality of the load.

    A dry van requires a raised dock for easy loading and unloading of cargo. Some dry vans are equipped with a lift gate that enables them to load and unload freight at ground level.

These trailers are common in the less-than-truckload carrying of cargo.

2. **Reefer**

A reefer is a square trailer. It has the same shape and capacity as a dry van. The difference is that a reefer boasts a refrigeration unit to maintain the temperature at certain levels. This is ideal for hauling food products that must be kept fresh by either freezing or heating.

So, a reefer must meet strict airflow regulations to maintain a set internal temperature irrespective of external weather changes. The refrigeration unit obtains power from a combination of truck power, batteries, and diesel. Because of the refrigeration unit and extra fuel, reefers take lighter loads than dry vans.

3. **Flatbed**

A flatbed is the second most common type of trailer in the U.S. trucking industry. It is the workhorse of the freight industry. Their design allows cargo to be loaded at the rear and via two lateral sides. Once loaded, bindings such as straps and chains fasten the cargo in place to prevent it from falling and getting damaged.

A closer look at the flatbed design reveals that it isn't flat throughout the deck. It bows along the length to support the freight weight without breaking. The flatbed fits transporting shipments to multiple destinations. The cargo headed the furthest could be loaded in the middle and the load that's going the nearest in the periphery. This helps to avoid damaging the shipments when loading and unloading.

4. **Step Deck**

The step deck is a variation of the flatbed. Its design allows it to easily carry taller loads. It consists of an upper-deck and a lower-deck. The upper deck's height is the same as the flatbed, while the lower-deck sits a foot and half lower. The lower deck occupies three-fourths of the trailer.

Should You Buy or Lease Trucks?

As a trucking start up business you have two options to own trucks. The first way is through the outright purchase of the vehicles. And the second approach uses the leasing method. Each of these has its pros and cons, and depends on your needs, circumstances, and financial muscles. For example, technology is advancing at a rapid rate in the trucking industry. Unfortunately, it's challenging to keep up with training and producing enough qualified technicians. As a result, you could own high tech trucks and struggle with maintenance.

Some trucking businesses choose to lease trucks, while others prefer to combine outright ownership with leasing. The decision depends on several factors, such as the type of freight you load, carrier lanes, seasonality, and type of trucks. So, it's helpful to understand how the two options differ so that you can make an informed decision.

Leasing Trucks

Leasing a truck means that you agree with a leasing company that it will provide the vehicle under the agreed terms. Then you pay a certain amount regularly (usually monthly). The amounts you usually pay do not cover the truck's full cost by the time the lease expires. At this time, you'll have various options as to how to proceed. We'll discuss this further below.

Leasing allows trucking companies to access equipment with no upfront costs and is helpful for owners with credit limitations. Often, you don't need to make any down payments. This is good because you can use the down payment elsewhere in the business, such as in marketing and promotion.

Today's trucks become obsolete quicker because of technological improvements. Leasing overcomes this challenge because it has shorter trade cycles and you can quickly upgrade to a fleet equipped with new technology.

Rental terms built into lease contracts can provide for increased capacity for seasonal work. When demand wanes, you can wind down capacity. Here's a list of top benefits of leasing:

- Trucking companies don't have to account for trucks in the balance sheet for certain kinds of leases.
- Gets rid of hidden costs involved in outright ownership of trucks.
- It frees you up to focus on key trucking business activities instead of things like maintenance.

- High truck running times because of regular preventative maintenance.

Types of Leases

Leases come in varying types to cater to different trucking business needs. It's important to know which one resonates with you to become as profitable as you want.

1. **Operating (Full-Service) Lease**

   In an operating lease, the leasing business maintains the trucks and also keeps its ownership. This frees the trucking company to focus on other operational measures like driver performance and customer satisfaction.

   There are various financing options with full-service leases. You can choose the term of the lease, financing arrangements, the type of truck, and your preferred level of maintenance. However, the operating lease doesn't suit all trucking businesses.

   It's vital to do a cost analysis and let numbers tell you whether this kind of lease is the right one or not. In other words, don't go by your gut or emotions to decide if this lease suits you or not.

   If you need specialized trucks and operate where you don't need priority service, then a full-service lease might not be a good option for your business.

2. Terminal Rental Adjustment Clause (TRAC) Lease

A terminal rental adjustment clause lease provides for altering payment terms and lengths and offering residuals while the contract is still in force.

A truck lease takes a portion of the vehicle's cost and distributes it to be paid monthly on equal installments. The payments include interest. At the end of the lease, the vehicle has an outstanding balance not covered by your monthly payments. This remaining balance of the vehicle cost is called a residual. The leasing company retains the vehicle ownership until the lease expires.

TRAC provides an opportunity to negotiate monthly payments and the residual. So, you can opt for a higher residual with lower monthly payments or vice versa. The actual monthly payments will depend on the truck cost and how you negotiate with the leasing company. Here's what the flexible term of this lease means to you.

You may end the lease after its minimum term lapses. At this point, the leasing company either purchases or sells the truck. The money from the sale pays the balance on the original cost of the truck. It's possible to receive a refund if the selling price fully covers the residual. Or you may owe the leasing company if the selling price is lower than the truck cost.

You also may choose to purchase the truck at the agreed-upon residual when the lease expires. But you do have a choice of whether to extend the lease or not.

That's how a basic TRAC lease works. There are three more varieties of the TRAC lease.

- **Split TRAC lease**: This lease is identical to the basic TRAC lease with one major difference. The split TRAC lease protects you against market volatility. If you have a shortfall at the sale of your truck, the most you'll pay doesn't go beyond a given maximum.

- **Zero TRAC lease**: Here, the leasing company adjusts the amortization schedule to leave a zero residual at the end of the lease. This means that you become the truck owner when the lease lapses, provided that you don't take the early termination option. This suits a trucking business owner who wants to own the truck after the lease.

- **Modified TRAC lease**: Recent accounting standards require TRAC leases to be classified as capital leases for tax purposes. This means that a truck appears on your business's balance sheet as an asset. In other words, the truck appears as if it is your own. A modified TRAC lease turns this situation around and turns the TRAC lease into an operating lease. This means the truck now becomes a business expense for tax purposes. Therefore, you need to choose a TRAC lease that gives you tax advantages. And you can determine this by considering how the numbers look on either lease type.

3. **Lease-Purchase Plans**

A lease-purchase plan is a kind of lease suitable for prospective truck owners who want to own their trucks without making a down payment. It's suitable for trucking business owners who don't have a sparkling credit history.

When you enroll in a lease-purchase program, you're classified as an owner-operator right away. Owners of the lease-purchase program may supply you with a steady supply of work for you to make lease payments.

It's essential to shop around for reputable and trustworthy lease-purchase programs because they offer different benefits. Where possible, enroll in a program like this:

- Doesn't charge hidden fees. In other words, the company running the program must be transparent about all the fees that you'll be charged. Also, read the contract fully to ensure you understand what you get yourself into.

- Offers discounts on things like fuel and shopping rates.
- Is less costly. This is important because it can cost $750 to $800 a week for older trucks or $1,100 to $1,200 to lease new vehicles. So, the lower the rates you find, the better your profits will be.

That's not all. There are lease-purchase programs that do not charge fees for Qualcomm, trailers, and cargo insurance. These businesses could result in lower expenses for your company and an improved profit position.

Let's now turn our attention to purchasing your own trucks.

Buying Your Own Trucks

Purchasing your own trucks gives you advantages that leasing does not. One great advantage is that it allows you to make significant tax deductions. It's no wonder two-thirds of trucking companies own their fleet as opposed to leasing. Perhaps some begin by leasing but do so with the intention of buying when the leases expire.

However, owning trucks brings with it several hidden costs. These are costs that you may not easily spot. They are:

- Running a maintenance workshop.
- Hiring maintenance technicians to maintain the fleet.
- Paying taxes and licensing.
- Purchasing truck consumables.
- Performing regular maintenance and attending to breakdowns.

With this in mind, it should be clear to you that, whether or not you choose to lease should be based on sound financial analysis. Business is a rational sport. If you run it primarily through emotions, you'll wind up making many mistakes. And then spend most of your time correcting these setbacks instead of moving the business forward.

When you buy trucks, they appear on your balance sheet as assets. And the loan you take becomes a liability on the same balance sheet. When you do your financial analysis to determine if leasing or purchasing is better, consider the following buying advantages:

- Buying allows you to depreciate the truck.
- Purchasing the truck affords you the luxury to deduct any interest you pay on the loan to buy the truck.
- You're permitted to deduct part or all of the money you used to buy the truck immediately. What does this mean, you may ask? Well, to

answer you, let me use an example. Let's say you buy a truck for $50,000 and its salvage value at the end of five years is $7,500. By the way, salvage value is the market value of your truck at a given point in its life. As the business owner, you're allowed to deduct $42,500 ($50,000 minus $7,500) the same year of the purchase of the truck. This is like getting paid to own the truck. And you can see why you should do a financial analysis before you decide to buy or not. Ensure that you use the current IRS Section 179 for the appropriate tax deduction.

Let's say after this matter of purchasing your own truck, you decide to buy. What financing options do you have to buy the truck(s)?

How to Finance the Purchase of Your Truck(s)

Most truck companies rely heavily on financing to buy their fleet. It's understandable because purchasing a truck requires a substantial amount of money. And most don't necessarily have the cash in hand or because financing makes financial sense. Unfortunately, like banks, traditional lending institutions often don't finance trucking companies, especially if they are still new. This means that you'll have to look for financing elsewhere.

Before you head out to look for financing, pay attention to the following:

- **Get it straight in your mind what exactly you want the funding for**. Do you want to purchase one truck or more? How much would it cost? How much financing do you want? The answers to these questions lie within the pages of your business plan. This document will play a major role in securing financing, as you'll see in a moment.

- **Know that borrowing costs money**. You may be charged an interest rate of about 5% if you have a clean credit record and a sound equipment plan. On the other hand, it's common to be charged 7% to 30% when your credit record isn't as clean.

One of the financing options that you have is commercial truck funding. The advantage of this sort of financing is that it is tailored to commercial trucking. So, you deal with funders who understand your needs.

Commercial Truck Financing

Like any funding, commercial truck financing has certain requirements that you must meet before you can get the funds. Let's go over each one of them.

1. **Personal Credit History**

   Your personal credit history plays a role in your successful application for commercial truck funding. It gives funders an idea of whether you're on top of your finances or not. In other words, it tells the funders how risky you are as the business owner. A high credit score means you're less risky. Thus, you may get lower interest rates and your chances of getting funding improves.

In contrast, a bad credit record signals that you're a higher risk when it comes to funding. And you may qualify for a higher interest rate. Or you may even not qualify for the funding.

Don't let your personal credit score alone block you from seeking funding. Why? Because there are other factors that financiers consider that may be favorable to you.

2. **Recent Personal and Business Credit Events**

As I said above, lenders often look at your personal credit history when applying for commercial trucking finance. They also do the same with your business credit record (if already available). Certain events can make your funding application a nightmare. Some of these include the following:

- Tax liens.
- Record of a high frequency of late payments.
- Bankruptcies.

Before you go out to look for the funds, obtain your latest credit record to check for incorrect information. If you find any, take steps to have it corrected by the credit agencies.

3. **Down Payment**

It's unlikely for commercial truck financing to cover 100% of the purchase price of the truck. Therefore, you may need to table a certain amount of down payment. The amount of down payment you have helps funders determine your seriousness, how much of a credit risk you are, and how risky a loan to you would be. The higher the down payment, the lower the risk to them and you're likely to get funding. Down payments often run from 5% to 30%.

4. **Cash in the Bank**

    The amount of money in your business bank is an indication of your money habits. If you have a substantial amount of cash in the bank, you're seen as responsible. Furthermore, the lenders will likely feel that you have the skills to manage risk and have more confidence in you. They would feel that you have the ability to make the required monthly repayments. And thus, you minimize the chance of them losing money.

5. **Relevant Business Documentation**

    Commercial truck financing lenders, like any lender, want to loan out money to legitimate entities. And the way to demonstrate that your business is legitimate is through supplying the following documents:

    - Tax returns (if applicable).
    - Licenses and permits.

- Financial statements, such as the balance sheet, cash flow statement, and the profit and loss statement.
- Copies of customer contracts and purchase orders (if any). Nothing proves that your business is sound than having customers.
- Bank statements.
- USDOT Number and MC number.

6. Business Track Record

The longer your trucking business's track record, the higher the chance of receiving funding. But it must be a track record that tells a good story about your business. At this point, you should be having a strong client base and a record that you deliver on your promises.

However, for a start-up, the business track record usually won't be something to write home about. So, your best bet is your business plan and any freight contracts that you may have garnered since beginning to operate. It's clear that as soon as you begin preparing to start your trucking business, you should be actively looking for customers at the same time. If you find contracts before being ready to deliver, you can hire another carrier to fulfill them for you for a fee.

7. Type of Truck(s) You Want to Buy

The type of truck presents its own risk to a lender. Used trucks cost less but are riskier to businesses than new ones. Furthermore, the truck's condition is vital because it should last at least until you have fully paid off the loan. Something else that's important is whether the truck will be doing short-haul or long-haul. The latter is riskier.

Vital truck information that you need to gather includes the following:

- Make and model of the truck.
- Mileage of the truck.
- Is it new or second hand?
- Complete condition report.
- Details of the truck seller.
- Warranties or certain assurances to minimize risk.

8. **Insurance**

Insurance is critical. Having an insurance quote for the truck indicates to the lenders that you're serious about buying it. This will likely improve your chances of getting the funds.

Small Business Administration(SBA) Loans

The Small Business Administration (SBA) partners with lenders on loans to small businesses. Notice that the SBA does not provide loans. What it does is set guidelines for loans offered by its lending partners to simplify access to funding while reducing risk for lenders.

Here are some benefits of loans backed up by the SBA:

- Some loans do not require collateral.
- You don't need to have large down payments.
- Competitive rates and fees.
- Some loan providers give business support to enhance your chances of success. If you think about it, this approach makes sense because the lender makes money when you succeed. It's a win-win situation.
- You're allowed to use the loan to buy long-term assets, such as trucks and buildings, and for operations.

The SBA loans start from as low as $500 to as high as $5.5 million. To access these loans, lenders look at several criteria, such as the following:

- The nature of the business and how it generates money.
- The kind of business ownership.
- The physical location of the business.
- The business must be registered and operating legally.
- You should be doing business and located in the U.S.
- The business owner must invest either sweat or cash equity in the company.
- The business is not allowed to source funds from any other lender.

As you can see, the requirements don't differ much from those of commercial trucking funding. If you prepare for your SBA funding as if you're going to apply for commercial truck financing, you'll improve your chances of success.

Business Line of Credit

A business line of credit works exactly like a personal credit card. It gives you access to revolving credit. This means that, if you qualify, you'll be allowed to borrow up to a specific limit. Once you have borrowed, you pay back the money, including interest. And then, you can again borrow from the total credit you have.

You don't have to borrow all the credit available. A positive thing about a business line of credit is that you pay interest only on your borrowed amount. This credit type suits short-term funding needs.

There are two types of business lines of credit. One kind is secured while the other is unsecured. The secured line of credit requires collateral. Typically, you'll use short-term assets, such as inventory as collateral. On the other hand, an unsecured line of credit tends to charge higher interest rates. To qualify, your business often should have a good track record and an unblemished credit profile.

To apply for a business line of credit is simple. All that is required is that you submit the following together with your application:

- Recent business bank statements.
- Tax returns.

- The latest financial statements.
- A business license.

Warning: The lender may call up the business line of credit anytime they want. At that point, you'll be asked to pay all the outstanding balance. Therefore, use the amount of credit that you know you'll be able to pay back on short notice.

Business Credit Card

A business credit card is designed specifically for company use. It is available for both small and large businesses. A credit card is an ideal tool to use if you want to build a business credit file.

Business credit card issuers may require backing through your personal guarantee. The way to apply for this credit card is the same as for a personal kind. You can get a business credit card from several institutions. Once again, shop around for better terms and interest rates. A 1% difference can make a massive difference in the amount of interest you pay.

Factoring

Factoring is a funding technique based on a business's future liquid assets like accounts receivable. This means that you can use assets like invoices to access funds on a short-term basis. Companies are willing to loan you money, at a fee, based on your liquid assets (excluding cash).

It is like these companies that buy your accounts receivable at a fee. The good thing is that they often pay you within 24 business hours after you deliver the load to the customer. Your customer then pays this sort of company from 30 to 35 days later.

The advantages of factoring include the ability for you to access money quickly. Also, you don't have to deal with individual customers about payments because you work with one factoring company. This saves you time for administration work. However, factoring can be costly because you may be charged from 3% to 5% of the load price, depending on its size.

If you decide to use a factoring company, choose one that is reputable and transparent with their fees and terms. You can obtain this information from other owner-operators who have been through the process before. Never sign any contract with a factoring company without studying it thoroughly. There may be something untoward in the contract which could land you into trouble later.

What's next now that you have a truck? It's time to run the trucking operations, and we tackle this topic next.

Chapter 5
Running Your Business

The manner in which you run your business determines its success or failure. So, you need ways to run your company successfully. And this begins with the right application of your business plan. It doesn't mean that you should follow the business plan to a tee even when things don't work. Your business plan serves as a starting point. And you'll tweak it where you deem necessary.

Hiring Reliable Truck Drivers

One of the most vital aspects of running a successful trucking business is to hire reliable and effective drivers. Even if you're an owner-operator, you still should hire a truck driver to swap time off. This would allow your truck to run more and make you more money. Furthermore, it's plain good business to have a relief driver because you need rest to be effective.

Finding good truck drivers in the United States isn't a walk in the park. The trucking industry suffers from one of the highest turnovers in the country. Smaller transporters have seen as high as a 73% driver turnover rate (Raphelson, 2018). So you need to have a water-tight recruiting process. Such a recruitment approach relies on thorough screening, hiring the right driver, followed by an effective orientation and onboarding process.

One tool to help in the driver hiring process is the Pre-Employment Screening Program (PSP) developed by the FCMSA. The system offers access to a commercial driver's safety record kept in the FMCSA Motor Carrier Management Information System (MCMIS). The data you'll find gives you a driver safety record in the previous five years. These records include any crashes or inspections in which the driver was involved. The inspections go back up to three years. This gives you confidence that you're hiring someone with a higher chance of driving safely.

Driver Qualities to Look for When Hiring

Besides the safety record of a driver, there are other qualities to look for. As you know, a human being is complex and cannot be defined by a single variable. Hence, you need to check for a lot more when hiring a truck driver, including the following:

- **Reliability**: Every hiring person requires reliable employees. You are no exception. A reliable driver assures you that they'll do what they promise. You can trust that they'll deliver customer goods at the agreed times. If they encounter problems along the way, they'll raise a flag and let you know if there are changes to the original plan.

- **Self-reliant**: A truck driver who will always want your help isn't a good employee. You want someone who would own the truck, make tough decisions, and continuously update their relevant knowledge. This is the kind of driver who you know will solve problems when they pop up, and they will.

- **Stress management skills**: The trucking industry is tough and, therefore, requires a tough-minded truck driver. Such individuals have the ability to manage the stresses accompanying the driving job.

- **Fitness**: A fit body doesn't get sick easily. Furthermore, a fit driver is able to handle stressful situations better than an unfit one. Also, a fit driver can work for long hours and still stay alert and drive safely.

- **Top driving record**: A driver who possesses an impeccable driving record gives you confidence that your customers' goods and truck are safe. So, they tend to be cheaper to insure, which helps improve your trucking business's profitability.

Once you know what kind of a driver you're looking for, it's time to go out and find them.

Where to Find Truck Drivers

There are several ways of finding good truck drivers. The high turnover in the industry means some drivers are looking for companies that can take good care of them. Here are some approaches to use to search for drivers.

- **Networking**: Contact people you know, such as friends and family members, and let them know that you're looking for a truck driver. It also helps to inform them what kind of a driver you're looking for. It will save you time, energy, and making a recruitment mistake.

- **Online marketing**: This approach requires you to post your driver requirements on social media. You could also create valuable information and post it on your website to attract your kind of drivers. This is called content marketing. Other approaches include email marketing and pay-per-click advertising.

- **Post truck driver jobs on call-to-action channels, such as online job boards**. You may also run newspaper ads targeted to your kind of driver.

- **Contact potential drivers directly**. Some drivers post their resumes on job boards. You may collect their details and contact them directly to see if they have what you want.

Many other ways open up immediately when you begin the search for drivers. When matching a truck driver with your business, always check for the following:

- That they are comfortable being away from home and family frequently.
- That they don't mind working a variable schedule.
- You need to be indirect with this one. If you want to hire a driver for the long-term, be mindful that this aspect also depends on how

you'll treat your driver. If you care for them, they'll likely care for you. We'll go deeper later when we talk about your retention strategy.

Truck Driver Salaries

Trucking companies often pay their drivers per mile covered. Different drivers get different wages based on experience, the kind of cargo they hail, qualifications, and where they drive. Standard rates start from $0.27 to $0.40 per mile (Roadmaster Drivers School, n.d.).

A typical driver covers anywhere from 2,000 to 3,000 miles per week. This means that you may expect to pay your drivers from $540 to $1,200 per week. However, keep in mind that the final amount will depend on your negotiations with the driver, as well as other benefits that you offer.

The good thing about paying per mile is that drivers push harder to cover more miles. They know that the more miles, the more money they'll make. Yours is to ensure that your drivers cover genuine and profitable miles.

How to Retain Your Truck Drivers

I've already alerted you on the high turnover in the trucking industry. Just imagine the impact a turnover like 94% has on large trucking companies. This means that you can spend a chunk of your time looking for drivers. And, after finding them, they leave within a short space of time. This is tragic. But you can improve your retention.

It starts with understanding why drivers change carriers so often. Then you can position yourself to be an employer of choice. And that process starts with recruitment. Hiring drivers that don't match your organizational culture is a sure means to a high driver turnover. That's not a good way of running a business because hiring and training drivers are costly. And, during the hiring process, you may not be able to use your full trucking capacity.

So, what should you include in your driver retention strategy? Here are five ways to keep drivers for longer.

1. **Respect and Appreciate Your Drivers**

   Most trucking businesses assume income and benefits can reduce driver attrition rates. If it were so, the problem of high driver turnover would have been nipped on the butt ages ago. So, there must be other factors involved.

   A 2019 Randall-Reilly truck driver poll discovered that 20% of truck drivers disliked their jobs because nobody appreciates what they do. In fact, they said that truck driving was a thankless job. Furthermore, 64% of them felt there isn't enough respect for truck drivers (Randall-Reilly & Commercial Carrier Journal, 2019).

   You can differentiate yourself by showing appreciation to all your employees all the time. It's even better if you make this part of your company DNA. One good way to show appreciation and respect is to prepare and send a weekly communiqué to your employees where you thank them for being part of your business.

2. **Set Achievable Job Expectations**

A Stay Days Table index from Stay Metrics revealed that 64.9% of truck drivers hired in the first quarter of 2019 worked beyond 90 days (Commercial Carrier Journal, 2019). These drivers said that knowing what's expected of them was crucial in the first few days or weeks on the job.

This means that, as a business owner, it's essential to inform your drivers, during recruitment, what their work schedule will be, their income, and the routes they'll travel. When you set these expectations, ensure that they're realistic to avoid drivers feeling like failures. Honestly, who wants to feel like a failure? I'm sure you and I don't, and we shouldn't expect others would like failing.

If you hire recruiters, tell them to be honest about the job and the company. Otherwise, when drivers find that what they were told isn't synonymous with what they see, they'll leave.

3. **Provide Driver Support**

The 2019 Randall-Reilly poll also found that 40% of drivers were concerned about government regulations and 37% worried about paying bills. Furthermore, drivers also rated spending time at home with family and their health as important.

These topics provide ample opportunity to write a weekly communiqué to your drivers and other employees. Your topics could include how drivers can stay healthy and explain how regulations benefit them and their families. As long as drivers see regulations as punishment, they're unlikely to comply, and this could hurt your business.

4. **Offer Attractive Pay**

When asked why trucking companies fail to attract drivers, 72% of the respondents in the Randall-Reilly poll said that transporters don't pay enough. Concerning was that 37% said if offered more money elsewhere, they would leave for another fleet.

It shows how important pay is to truck drivers. And you cannot afford not to pay a competitive wage. You can do this by offering a respectable amount of regular and guaranteed mileage at a good pay per mile. Also, you could offer health and retirement packages to reduce financial weight on your drivers.

5. **Introduce Driver-Benefit Technology**

Technology, like dash cams, can help improve driver productivity and safety. Of course, drivers, like everyone else, like to be trusted. Unfortunately, technology like this could make drivers feel like they're not trusted.

So, install technology that provides drivers with clear benefits and make that a reason for its use. But do ensure that this technology improves productivity at the same time. That way, you have a technology that delivers a win-win for both company and driver.

A good example is installing satellite T.V. and radio. These gadgets entertain your drivers and can help them reduce stress. Less stress means better problem-solving and, therefore, better performance. And improved performance makes your business profitable.

The Need for Other Employees

Life has a way of getting in the way. You may face life's curveballs and that may stop the operation of your business in your absence. You may also want to grow your business, and it won't be possible if you're all alone in the company.

So, you may need to hire other employees to help with a variety of business tasks. Yes, you may decide to outsource some tasks like legal or bookkeeping, but you may not have the time to hold these third parties accountable in the event they don't deliver proper work. For this reason, hire at least one other employee to help you answer phones and handle your business records, such as accounting.

The way you hire any employee involves implementing savvy recruitment strategies. Hire them like you are looking for a business partner. Aren't they your business partner? They are because their livelihood will depend on the success of your business.

How to Find Paying Customers

If there's any most important task in your business, it is to find paying customers. This is so for a good reason. Customers are the lifeblood of any trucking business. There's no cash flow without customers. To keep having customers and positive cash flow, it is helpful to diversify.

It's important to solicit customers who pay high rates per load. This helps your business become profitable without having to cover thousands and thousands of miles. But finding customers can be tough, not only for trucking businesses but for any business. Your ability to find good-paying loads will determine your business's success or failure.

At this point, you would have given thought to who your ideal customer is when creating your business plan. What's left is to take action and find them. But how will you find them? We'll get to that in a moment. Let's first look at what kind of a shipper is the right customer for a trucking company.

This criterion is general in nature. Yours would be more specific but cover these qualifications as well. Here's what to look for in an idea shipper:

- They pay well and on time.
- The shipper supplies loads regularly.
- They're an established and reputable shipper.
- The customer offers loads that match your freight lanes.

Armed with that customer information, you head out to look for them using one or more of the following ways.

Six Ways of Finding Customers

It's now time to find customers who will bring revenue to your business. There are several ways of doing this. But we'll go over seven powerful ones here.

1. Networking at Industry Associations

To access members of industry associations often requires you to join the organization. It's not every association that has your customer. Choose industry associations you know your ideal customers belong to. For example, if your customer is in retail, then look at joining retail associations. If in contraction, you join construction associations and so on.

Some industry associations welcome corporate members. You can use this opportunity to join and network with your ideal shippers. In the process, you'll be able to see how you can serve them. Your big idea is not to sell your services but to collect connections and leads. Business leads are people you can potentially serve. Don't try to sell because the environment isn't conducive to deals involving large sums of money. Consultative selling is a better approach to getting trucking business.

Consider creating an industry report beneficial to your ideal customers. Then you can offer it to your customers in exchange for their contact details. That way, you add value to them and their business immediately. Furthermore, this approach sets you apart from your competitors and establishes you as an authority.

Later, get in touch with your newly-acquired contacts to set up meetings where you'll sell them your services.

Another option is to get a list of members of a given association. Then send the members your report to establish the first contact. A few days later, you may contact them to check if they received the report. That then provides you an easy start to a selling process. The standard rate directory service list book also provides an option to obtain lists of your targeted associations' lists.

2. **Register with Government as a Contractor**

The government hires many small businesses for various services and products. You can access regular work from the government, and they're often reliable on payments. With many government departments and agencies, there are ample opportunities to provide a trucking service.

What you need to do is register with the government as a vendor. Search for relevant business opportunities using keywords and other criteria like locations. Then review selected opportunities to understand what the government wants and what their terms are.

If you are interested in a job, all you do is prepare a bid at competitive prices while staying profitable. Finally, submit your bid and wait for the decision on who gets awarded the contract.

It's advisable to start bidding for government work at the local level. This will help you understand the government's procurement processes, so you become efficient and bidding and project delivery. If you get a larger contract, you may have to source extra funding to be able to complete the job in time. But this is an easier problem to solve because you can request funds from factoring companies.

3. **Hire a Freight Broker**

   Freight brokers connect shippers to carriers and make money in the process. Getting the services of a broker is a good strategy for a trucking business start up. They do most of the work, such as negotiating rates with shippers.

   However, you should be aware that you'll likely be paid lower rates than directly working shippers. Still, ensure that they pay you more than your cost per mile. And ensure that there are no hidden fees by studying the contract thoroughly.

4. **Use Truck Dispatcher Services**

   There are freight dispatchers that also offer load finding services to trucking companies. They charge either a fixed amount or on a pay per load basis. This option suits startup businesses like yours because you don't have a profitable list of clients yet.

5. **Online Marketing**

   Online marketing refers to initiatives you do online to get paying customers. There are many ways to do online marketing, including content marketing, email marketing, pay-per-click advertising, and social media marketing. If you don't have online marketing skills, don't jump into using them because you could make costly mistakes. First, familiarize yourself with your chosen online marketing approach to avoid losing time and money.

6. **Use Load Boards**

We've spoken about this when working out what to quote brokers and shippers. In the beginning, opt for free load boards if you can't afford paid versions.

7. **Personal Prospecting**

Personal prospecting involves conducting research to find shippers in your location. Then, you check what kind of goods they ship and to where. If they carry cargo that runs on your lane, you get in touch with them and ask for a short meeting over coffee or lunch.

In the meeting, focus on asking questions about their business. Begin with the general and drive to the specifics relating to shipping. In the process, you'll discover how your business could be of better service to them.

Don't use all the above techniques to find customers. Select two or three, and work them. You're welcome to swap one with another if it doesn't deliver the results you want. However, remember to be patient.

How to Price Your Freight

It costs money to transport cargo from one point to the next. You cannot afford to transport the load at a higher cost than the pay you receive. It's impossible to build a thriving business that way. A trucking business should be able to fund itself with the cargo that it transports.

Therefore, to run a profitable trucking business requires that you know your revenue and expenses. Here's how to figure out your cost per mile.

1. **Compute the Total Mileage**

   The mileage a truck covers determines how much the shipper pays for a given type of load. Different truck drivers cover varied mileages per month. These mileages include both paid and unpaid (called deadhead) distances. The average truck driver covers about 8,400 miles a month. I'll use this figure to illustrate our calculations as I proceed with working out the cost per mile.

2. **Determine Your Fixed Expenses**

   The business costs that you'll incur fall into either the fixed or variable expense category. Fixed costs stay the same from one month to the next irrespective of the amount of work you do. For example, monthly license fees and truck payments stay unchanged.

   Some fixed costs get paid annually and therefore should be distributed monthly for our purposes here. Let's assume that the cost of a given permit is $1,800 per year. That works out to $150 per month ($1,800/12).

3. **Compute Your Variable Expenses**

Unlike fixed costs, variable expenses often change monthly. The actual amount due to a variable cost depends on the mileage you drive. When you cover a large distance, the cost will be higher and vice versa. Examples of variable costs include fuel, maintenance, and meal expenses.

Suppose your fuel cost is $0.55 per mile. Over a month when you cover 8,400 miles, you'll spend $4,620 ($0.55 x 8,400) on fuel. In a month when the truck drives 6,300, the fuel cost works out to $3,465.

4. **Figure Out the Cost Per Mile**

Now, divide the total fixed cost by 8,400 to find the fixed expenses per mile. For example, if your total fixed cost is $5,620, then the fixed expense per mile will be $0.67 ($5,620/8,400).

Using the same approach, calculate your variable cost per mile. A total variable cost of $2,350 leads to $0.28 per mile.

To determine the total cost per mile, simply add the fixed cost per mile to the variable expenses per mile. The total cost per mile is $0.95 ($0.67 + $0.28) in the example used above.

Alternatively, you can add the total fixed and variable costs and divide the outcome by 8,400 like this: $7,970 ($5,620 + $2,350) divided by

8,400 to get $0.95. This means that you cannot quote below $0.95 per mile per load and still be profitable. To make your calculations easy, use this **spreadsheet**. All you do is insert appropriate numbers in the spreadsheet and it will effortlessly compute the cost per mile for you. But there's more to consider in your pricing.

What Else to Include in Your Pricing

A freight delivery cost depends on three components, namely, linehaul, fuel surcharge, and accessorials. Let's go over each so you can have a better understanding of these terms.

- **Linehaul**: This is the cost to carry a shipment from its origin to the destination. The distance covered determines the total expense. The calculation we did above was linehaul. Linehaul for LTL and parcels varies based on the weight or volume the load occupies in the trailer. The larger the weight or volume, the more the linehaul.

- **Fuel surcharge**: When a trucker buys fuel, they get charged fuel tax. So, truckers include an additional fuel charge in their prices to hedge against diesel fuel fluctuations. This extra fuel charge is called the fuel surcharge.

Fuel surcharge can be added either as a percentage of the linehaul cost of cost per mile. Truckers use fuel data from the weekly (on

Tuesdays) updated U.S. Energy Information (EIA) website.

- **Accessorials**: Beginner truckers often make the mistake of excluding accessorials in the load prices. These are charges added to the shipment cost for any extra work or time the trucker puts into the shipment, often excluded in the originally agreed price.

Three Shipment Pricing Methods

There are three shipment pricing methods depending on the work to be done and the trucker's preference. The choice of pricing method affects the loading costs. The methods include spot, contract, and project pricing.

1. **Spot Pricing**

   Spot pricing is a method where negotiated prices depend on trucks and loads' current supply and demand. As a result, this pricing method is volatile. You can use this type to fill up trucking capacity to avoid deadhead miles or idle vehicles.

2. **Contract Pricing**

   Contract prices are shipment costs based on future volumes and shipper requirements. The price often stays the same over a twelve-month period. But bear mind that there is no guarantee you'll carry loads daily. So, it's essential to have multiple contracts to increase the utilization of your freight capacity.

The agreement between the shipper and carrier provides for loading when the trucker has capacity.

3. **Project Pricing**

Finally, there is project pricing, where negotiated prices follow the contract approach. However, project prices are valid for shorter periods.

Pricing Strategies in the Trucking Industry

The competition for loads is tight in the trucking industry. With increasing transportation costs, it's essential to use profitable pricing strategies to become and stay profitable. Successful trucking businesses tend to have similar pricing strategies. For example, they charge freight prices commensurate with the value of their services and products.

So, you must commit to profitable pricing approaches if you want to be profitable. Most importantly, never allow sales representatives (if you have any) to adjust your prices.

You can either use static or dynamic pricing. Dynamic pricing gives a price advantage. The change in prices comes from altering delivery areas; the products delivered, varying demand, and the economic environment. This approach allows you to tailor your prices to stay profitable. Let's go over three variations of dynamic pricing.

1. **Revenue Management Pricing**

Revenue management pricing is common with less-than-truckload (LTL) truckers. Prices reflect destinations and optimization based on the proportion of a truckload occupied by the shipper's load.

This strategy allows shippers to price their services based on full truckload irrespective of their product occupies' space.

2. **Yield Management Pricing**

   The yield management pricing strategy sets prices to reflect the need for quick and timely delivery of freight. This approach works well for carriers who transport perishable products.

   The quoted prices take into account changing established routes and swapping drivers to meet the delivery time requirement.

3. **Geographic Pricing**

   In geographic pricing, the prices mirror changes in fuel costs, the truck's wear and tear, and the driver's wages. Long-haul companies favor this kind of pricing because they can optimize their revenue.

   A popular example of utilizing this approach is called zone pricing. Here, prices differ based on geographic locations, that is, distance from shipping point to destination.

Those are the main approaches to dynamic pricing you could use. However, you may opt to do uniform pricing. This strategy applies the same prices for all shippers. Although less common, short-haul and local delivering companies use it

Four Tips to Negotiate Freight Rates

Would you like to get the best rates on load boards? How would you like to know a technique that helps swell your company's bottom line? Whether you're new in the trucking industry or are a new owner-operator, you should negotiate freight rates.

The keyword is 'negotiate.' Why? Because not all loads, especially those on load boards, include added transport fees like accessorials. Also, freight brokers may give themselves way higher markups and hurt you in the process.

Savvy negotiations require preparation and knowledge. Here are four ideas to consider when you plan to negotiate freight rates.

1. **Understand Your Operating Costs**

   Your operating cost is the expense you pay to haul a load for one mile. We've covered how to compute this figure earlier in the book. As we said, this figure is crucial because you can't run a profitable business unless your freight loads pay more than your cost per mile.

   Importantly, knowing your cost per mile allows you to set negotiation limits on freight rates to accept. Additionally, your cost per mile gives you an indication of where to anchor your freight prices. Anchoring is a process of setting a price's frame of reference. The higher, but reasonable, the anchoring price, the greater the chance of getting a larger price.

2. **Check Load Rates for Round-Trips**

Certain areas pay low freight rates. For example, freights to Florida often pay well. But the return journeys don't pay good rates. Armed with this knowledge, you can negotiate higher round-trip rates instead of focusing only on individual lanes. Although this approach is uncommon, it gives you the opportunity to avoid deadhead.

If you can't have a round-trip, then negotiate a higher rate to a destination and opt for a breakeven return leg to stay profitable. But try to avoid taking frequent low-paying lanes because it's a habit that can hurt your business severely.

3. **Select Loads with High Load-to-Truck Ratios**

A high load-to-truck ratio signifies that the demand for trucks is high relative to available loads. This provides you with room for negotiating prices as opposed to a low truck-to-load rate. Shippers become desperate to have their loads delivered. This is good for your trucking business.

4. **Notice the Load's Times**

Sometimes loads stay on the load board for long periods. This may cause shippers or brokers to start getting anxious and frustrated. This is the exact time when you chip in and offer your trucks.

The way to get these opportunities is to note the times loads spend on the load boards. When you see a particular load staying on the board for far too long, you call the shipper or broker and make yourself available to take it. That's when negotiations will begin.

The shorter the window is to pick-up time, the more shippers and brokers fret and are willing to negotiate. The hours of work for truck drivers combined with load timings provide a ripe chance to negotiate better freight rates.

When you negotiate, try to ask as many questions around the load as possible. The more the shipper or broker speaks, the more chance they give you to spot weaknesses and opportunities to argue for higher rates.

Not many business owners are fond of negotiating. This gives you an unfair advantage if you make up your mind to make negotiating part of your business strategy. Negotiating isn't a life and death action. The worst thing that can happen is hearing a 'no.' And when you hear this little word, you simply move back to the load board and other freight sources.

Once the negotiations reach their conclusion, ensure that you get agreed rates (including surcharges) and terms in writing before taking the load. This will help you avoid costly misunderstandings later on. Most important, before you load, do credit checks on the broker or shipper to eliminate the chance of working with bogus people and companies.

Scheduling and Fleet Management

Running a fleet effectively requires you to manage driver scheduling, truck maintenance and associated records, and driver training plans. You have two options available for this important task. You may choose to do it manually or through a fleet management software. The latter offers an easier and more efficient approach to fleet management and it's the approach I recommend.

Once set up, fleet management software provides ways to print copies of various reports for filing as required by various regulations such as IFTA taxes. You don't have to enter every data point and do calculations manually. The system works its computing magic in the background. And all you do is feed it a few numbers from which these different reports will be created.

Using this system allows you to optimize route plans and deliver freights on time. As you can tell, fleet management software helps minimize operational expense, improve driver productivity, and jerk up your business's profitability.

How Many Hours Should Truck Drivers Work?

Truck drivers aren't allowed to drive for as long as they want because it can be unsafe for themselves and other road users. So, some laws and regulations help ensure truck drivers work a given amount of time.

The FMCSA sets the hours of work for truck drivers. Interstate driving is subject to federal regulations. Here are some of those regulations that truck drivers should adhere to:

- Truck drivers are allowed to work only 60 hours over seven successive days or 70 hours over an eight-day duration. To manage these hours, a driver must keep a log for seven days and eight days thereafter.
- Drivers are allowed to work for up to 14 hours after being off duty for 10 hours. Of the 14 hours, 11 must be for driving.
- A driver must get a 30-minute break eight hours after coming on duty.
- Breaks, meals, and fuel stops are excluded in the 14-hour duration.

However, there's an Adverse Driving Condition exception that gives drivers an additional two hours of driving. This happens provided the driver experiences traffic delays due to construction, adverse weather, and traffic incidents.

There's also a 16-hour exception rule that applies to drivers on a one-day work schedule. Such drivers are allowed to work for 16 hours if they start and end their work at the same terminal.

Penalties for Violating Hours of Service (HOS) Rules

Like any government rule, a truck driver or transporter gets punished for violating the hours of service. The severity of the penalty or fine will depend on the kind and seriousness of the offense. Here's what may happen when a driver breaks the working hours rules:

- If your drivers work beyond allowable hours, they may be stopped by the roadside until they accumulate enough of a rest period to comply once more. State and local relevant officials may assess applicable fines.
- FMCSA may penalize your business and driver a fee ranging from $1,000 to $11,000 per infringement based on the severity of the violation.
- Your company's safety rating may be downgraded if you rack up a pattern of violations.
- The Federal law enforcement officials can charge you civil penalties if they find you knowingly allowed the infringement. The same could apply to your drivers.

Other Government Regulations to Comply With

There are other government regulations that your business should adhere to for trouble-free trucking. Let's talk about four important ones.

1. **Drug Testing**

   It's mandatory to test truck drivers for drugs and alcohol. Any driver who tests positive (verified) must be removed from their work immediately. If found adulterated, they should suffer the same consequences. A driver who refuses drug and alcohol testing must be removed from safety-sensitive tasks.

A trucking company must report its drug testing results to the government.

2. Engine Idling

Strange as it may sound, not all states and municipalities allow drivers to idle their engines.

Some who do allow engine idling give drivers a few minutes. Running the engine beyond that period may attract fines up to $25,000 (Trucking Job Finder, n.d.).

3. Weight Limit

Heavy vehicles can damage public roads faster than their lighter counterparts. For this reason, states and cities place a weight limit on trucks that carry cargo. So, it's important to familiarize yourself with these limits to avoid fines and penalties.

Usually, a truck found to be over the weight limits while carrying cargo may be stopped until another trailer reduces the load. This, obviously, will delay your truck and affect your profitability.

4. Safety Audits

The government requires truck companies to undergo a safety audit in the first 12 months of starting their operations. So, your business must avail itself for this audit or risk the FMCSA revoking their registration. This is because the safety audit is part of the process of getting a permanent operating authority.

Technology to Include in Your Truck

Certain technological devices help your drivers and company to comply with government rules and regulations. I'll discuss with you two of them.

- **Electronic logging device (ELD)**: An ELD is a device to track a driver's driving time and record duty status. As I explained earlier, you need to track your driver's hours of service. And this instrument ensures that you comply with the U.S. ELD mandate.

  The ELD you choose must be registered with and self-certified with the FMCSA. The ultimate goal of the ELD is to assist in creating a safer work environment for drivers. Additionally, an ELD simplifies fleet management.

- **Global Positioning System (GPS)**: A GPS is a device that helps you monitor the speed your trucks travel while on the road. As you know, a high speed increases the chances of accidents. A GPS may influence your drivers to drive at the right speeds. But you should be careful about using the GPS to monitor your trucks' speeds because drivers dislike being micromanaged.

- **Cam dash**: A dash camera helps drivers improve visibility and potentially reduce driving incidents. Therefore, it lowers the cost associated with truck accidents. If involved in a truck accident, the cam dash may exonerate your driver with video footage. Also, a cam dash simplifies insurance claims.

Truck Maintenance

Well-maintained trucks can help your driver stay safe while lowering operating costs. As a result, maintaining your trucks is a way to improve the profitability of your business. Here are some maintenance tasks you should do on your trucks.

- Do regular engine oil and filter changes. If possible, replace the filter with the type recommended by the manufacturer. A quick check into the truck's user manual should furnish you with the frequency of oil and filter changes.
- Check engine coolant, power steering fluid, windshield washer, and brake fluid level prior to taking a journey.
- Regularly rotate your tires to avoid uneven wear. This also helps to lengthen the service the tires give you.
- Inspect the exterior of the truck for any signs of damage.
- Acquire the services of an expert to inspect your trucks at least annually.
- Check to ensure the temperature control unit's proper functioning, accuracy and calibration of the temperature monitoring instruments.

- Inspect the insulation, floor grooves, and drains.
- Check proper operation of the interior and exterior lights, mirrors, brakes, battery, and steering.

With a sound truck, you could see more life and performance from it.

Join Trucking Associations

Joining trucking associations has different benefits than becoming a member of your customer associations. You join trucking associations to become updated with developments within the industry and regulatory changes. In addition, you also expand your network, an important resource for building a trucking business.

One of the organizations to consider joining is the American Trucking Association. One of its main reasons for existence is to help members operate safely while being profitable. Besides staying current with industry developments, you'll access business growth initiatives like conferences and education.

Take time and research trucking associations that you can join at the state level. Also, consider joining specialized associations such as the Truckload Carriers Association.

Alright. That brings us to the end of running your business. Now, let's turn our attention to managing your business's finances, a crucial part of running a thriving trucking business.

Chapter 6
Managing Your Business's Finances

It may be a cliché but the following idea carries power if you run a successful trucking business. That idea is this: you cannot manage it if you can't measure it. This thought also applies to managing your business finances. Therefore, it is imperative to determine early on what you'll measure to ensure your business succeeds. Fortunately, others have already walked this path. This means that you don't have to reinvent the wheel but simply learn what they've measured to manage a business's finances. I'll take you through the things involved in business accounting and financial management in a moment.

First, let's go over the process you need to follow to build an emergency fund. We talked earlier in the book about the value of having an emergency. Now, let's build it.

A Business Emergency Fund

As the name suggests, an emergency fund serves to finance your business costs in case there's an emergency. It follows that you should define events that fall into the emergency category. By definition, an emergency is an unforeseen occurrence often unprepared for things like a fire that licks your truck. Or your truck's refrigeration unit breaking down unexpectedly. Normally, an emergency in your trucking business can stop the operations.

Some businesses elect to use either a credit card or business line of credit to fund such emergencies. That's fine as long as they pay them before their bankers add interest. But if they wait until after the addition of interest, they end up overpaying and reducing their businesses' profitability, and this isn't good business management.

To avoid this difficult situation, why not create an emergency fund? When faced with an emergency, you simply whip out your debit card and pay for your refrigeration unit's repairs. The good thing with having cash is that you can negotiate lower costs far easier than using a credit line. Thus, your business profitability stays unaffected. And you experience less stress, a good thing for a business.

How to Build an Emergency Fund

Like anything else, creating and building an emergency fund takes initiative and the willingness to sacrifice. Most importantly, you should set it as a goal achievable within a given time period. Here are the steps, in sequence, to take to build an emergency fund.

1. **Set the goal amount you need to accumulate**. The amount of your emergency fund should cover three to six months of your business expenses. The time period provides you with ample time to return to normal operations. This means that if you spend $7,500 per month, your emergency fund should be

between $22,500 (3 x $7,500) and $45,000 (6 x $7,500).

These numbers may seem large, and they are. That's why when you have this fund you can have peace of mind. Remember that you're going to build this fund like building a house. You're going to take it one step at a time like we're doing now.

I'll use the lower figure of $22,500 to illustrate the process as we proceed. In other words, the emergency fund goal is to save $22,500.

2. **Decide on the target date to have set up the fund**. Setting a target date adds a bit of urgency. It works like a deadline to complete a task. When there's no deadline, what does a person normally do? Procrastinate, isn't it? And setting a target date eliminates this tendency to delay taking action.

For our purpose, I'll take it we're going to finish building this fund in 12 months. There's something else we're going to use this period for. It's going to help us figure out how much to set aside monthly.

3. **Work out how much to save monthly**. This is simple to do. Take your target emergency fund and divide it by the period to build the fund. In this case, I take $22,500 and divide it by 12. And the outcome is $1,875. This means that the

business should put aside, in a special fund, $1,875 monthly for emergency purposes.

Before we talk about where to get the money to save, let me address this question, "What happens if the business faces an emergency while still building the fund?" Well, to be frank, you use the money that's available. It is the cheapest money you'll ever have to handle financial emergencies. But that means you'll have to start afresh from there and rebuild the fund.

Alright. Let's carry on with an emergency fund-building process.

4. **Spend less than the business makes**. This isn't easy, especially if you aren't getting better freight rates. You should because if you don't, your business stands a small chance of succeeding.

   Other ways to save costs include buying fuel at lower prices. I'll explain how to do this later in this chapter. Another option is to negotiate almost every business expense you incur. Any saving you make goes into the emergency fund.

5. **Earn more money**. When earning more money, you should keep your fixed costs the same. Thus, you'll be able to build a larger cushion between your income and expenses and save more. This requires discipline. It's

hard, but the rewards, as often said, are worth it.

Ways to earn more money include getting more profitable loads. The way to do this is by chasing after high-paying freight. It may not be that easy. But committing to building the emergency fund forces you to push hard to obtain those high-paying loads.

That's all there is to building an emergency fund. As you can see, it requires you to manage your finances while getting paying customers. Let's go ahead and look at the actual task of managing your business's finances.

Business Accounting

The mark of a successful trucking business is how well the owner keeps financial and operational numbers. It's like keeping a business scorecard. This means that the numbers will inform you whether you're winning or losing. You could then make informed decisions that help you stay on track to achieve your business goals.

Business accounting involves capturing financial numbers that feed a variety of reports. These reports are called financial statements, and they serve a variety of functions. I'll get to them in a moment.

There are important accounting terms that you should be familiar with. Let's go over them briefly.

1. **Assets**: An business asset is something that a business owns. It can be physical or intellectual. Some common assets are buildings, trucks, cash in the bank, and inventory.

2. **Liabilities**: A business liability is anything that your company owes. In short, a liability is a debt. Good examples of liabilities are a truck loan and taxes.

3. **Equity**: An equity is what remains when the value of liabilities is taken out of the value of assets. In formula form, here's how accountants represent it:

$$Equity = Assets - Liabilities$$

As the equation suggests, when the value of liabilities exceeds that of the assets, you have negative equity. It means that the business owes someone. This is not a good space to be in.

As a business owner, you'll have a share of your company's ownership. If you are the sole owner, then all the business equity is yours. But if you own 60% of the business, then your equity is also 60%.

4. **Revenue**: When a business trades, it makes money. All that cash that comes into the business is termed revenue or gross revenue. Accountants often report revenue generated over a given period, such as monthly, half-yearly, or annually.

5. **Gains**: At times, you may sell some of your assets to generate quick cash. This income will result in a one-time increase in gross revenue. Such income is called a gain.

6. **Expenses**: This is self-explanatory, isn't it? An expense is a cost that the business incurs to run its operations.

7. **Losses**: Sometimes, you may sell a business asset at a cost less than the price you paid to acquire it. The difference between these two numbers is called losses.

The terms above are critical when analyzing financial statements. And it's essential to know the purpose of each of these financial statements. You cannot manage the finances of a business without using these vital reports. A simple search online can give you access to templates for preparing each of these major financial statements. Here's a short introduction to each of the main financial statements.

1. **Balance sheet**: A balance sheet is also called a statement of financial position. It gives the financial standing of a business at a particular point in time. Businesses use this statement to capture their assets, liabilities, and equity. Its main job is to show you the overall health of your business.

2. **Income statement**: This statement reports on the income the business generates as well as the expenses. It usually covers a given period, such as monthly, quarterly, or annually. This means that if you want to know whether your business is profitable or not, you use the income statement.

3. **Cash flow statement**: A cash flow statement captures the amount of cash the business possesses and projects future money movements (cash flows). It shows the day-to-day financial health of a business. It's a key statement because, without readily available cash, a business can battle to pay operational expenses. And if a business runs out of cash, it may fail despite the income statement showing a profit.

Those are the three major financial statements that you should be able to read and understand. Above all, you should be able to use them to make savvy business decisions.

Now, armed with the knowledge of key accounting terms and financial statements, you need to know the actions to take to generate their numbers. That's an important job. As you know, the kind of financial data you gather will determine the usefulness of your financial statements.

Capturing financial numbers can be done in one of two ways. You may choose to do it manually or through accounting software. I'm not a fan of manually creating financial statements because it takes time and is prone to errors. Instead, I prefer using an accounting system that requires punching in a few numbers and letting the technology do its magic behind the scenes. This saves time and allows you to focus on your core operations, like finding better paying freight loads.

An accounting system ideally suits a startup because you can easily run your business without accounting personnel or an accounting department. What's key is selecting the right accounting system. What do I mean by an accounting system? Let me explain.

You can run your business accounting functions based on either the accrual or cash-based system. The difference between the two systems is the timing of when the business receives cash. A cash-based system records income when the business receives money. Expenses get logged only when cash leaves the company. This system suits simple operations, such as for a small business where tracking of cash flow is vital.

In contrast, an accrual system captures revenue when the business earns it even if the money is not yet in the bank. For example, immediately you deliver a shipper's load, the price the customer should pay gets recorded as revenue. The same applies to expenses. They get logged into the system even before the actual cash exits the company. This system often works well for large corporations with resources to handle its complexity.

For the accounting system you choose to use to be effective, you'll regularly maintain your books. You want to feed the necessary numbers, if possible, daily or as soon as you have them. And it should be easy when you use accounting software because you enter a few numbers. This helps keep your financial numbers up to date and allow you to know on a daily basis where your business is going.

Any receipts you get should be kept safe for the IRS and state fuel tax purposes. One cool idea is to make digital copies of the receipts and keep them into your computer. Don't forget to regularly backup your computer to avoid loss of your business data due to things like theft or fire.

Monitoring Business Expenses

As we've discussed earlier in this book, your business has fixed costs such as truck payments, loan payments, payroll, and truck insurance. I also made you aware of the importance of determining your cost per mile. Doing this required not only the fixed costs but also your variable expenses. The numbers that you generated in this process form your operating budget. You may already know from your personal life that a budget is crucial for financial success. So it is for a small business like yours.

Your budget is the baseline from which to measure the effectiveness of your business financial management tasks. You should know whether you're running your company on a budget, below budget, or above budget over a given period.

One of the major expenses that can result in the above budget operations is fuel costs. It's not unusual to spend $4,000 per month on diesel (CDL.com, n.d.). As you already know, fuel cost is but one of the variable expenses. Others include tires and truck maintenance. The main reason for monitoring each of your expenses is to ensure your business stays profitable.

Since fuel costs make up a major portion of your business budget, it's necessary to discuss it in detail. Unlike regular drivers, truck drivers pay fuel taxes on the diesel they buy and use in each state. And the cheapest diesel is not based on the pump price. So, you need to understand how fuel prices and taxes work to come up with a cost-effective fuel-buying strategy. Not only will this strategy help you buy fuel cost-effectively, but it can also guide your route planning.

What's the Best Fuel-Buying Strategy

The buying of fuel for trucks can be confusing to new truck owners. Ridding this confusion requires an understanding of how fuel pricing works.

Each state charges a different price and tax for fuel. IFTA requires you to pay tax to each state you drive through, irrespective of where you buy the fuel. So, you pay for the fuel used in each of the jurisdictions you drove through. To simplify this process, let me show you how the IFTA taxes get calculated.

How to Calculate IFTA Taxes

To do this exercise, all you need are your fuel receipts, state to state miles you traveled, and current IFTA rates obtainable on their website. Armed with this information, this is what you do, step by step.

1. Compute the total mileage you covered during the reporting quarter. All you do is add the mileages covered in each state together. Your GPS or ELD can furnish you with this data.

2. Add up the gallons of fuel from your receipts to obtain the total you used during the quarter.

3. Determine the miles you covered per gallon of fuel. Simply divide the answer from step 1 by the answer from step 2 above.

4. Now, for each state, work out the gallons that you burned in that state. Simply multiply the

answer in step 3 above by the mileage you covered in a state. You do this calculation for each state you traveled through during the reporting quarter.

5. Calculate, using the latest IFTA rates, the fuel tax to pay for each state. All you do is multiply the answer in step 4 above by the IFTA tax rate for that state.

6. Now, compute the tax you've already paid to each state when fueling your truck. This requires multiplying the total fuel bought in the state by the state's IFTA tax rate.

7. Calculate the amount of fuel tax you owe in each state by subtracting the answer in step 6 from the answer in step 5 above. Some taxes will be negative while others positive. Your total IFTA tax is the sum of the fuel tax for each state.

8. Finally, you do the IFTA tax filing.

That's all there is to the process of figuring out the amount of IFTA tax to pay.

Because of the different state fuel taxes, you cannot use pump prices to tell which jurisdiction sells diesel cheaper. Instead, you must work out the base price of fuel per state. By the way, the base price is simply the difference between pump price and fuel tax. For example, let's say the diesel price in Colorado is $2.174 and the fuel tax rate is $0.2050 for each gallon you buy, respectively. Then, the base price will be $2.174 minus

$0.2050 which equals $1.969 a gallon. This latter price we've figured out is the base diesel price in Colorado.

So, it's important to know the states that you'll pass through when you deliver your freight. Then, work out the state that charges the lowest base price. Once done, you can plan your routes so buy diesel in that state.

There is another way you could pay lower fuel prices.

Use Reward Cards

Rewards cards are credit cards that offer fuel rewards when you fill fuel at a gas station. Some reward cards can offer you 3% cashback when you buy fuel at given gas stations. This means that if you buy fuel worth $500, you'd be rewarded with $15 cashback. This may not sound like much. But if you spend $4,000 on fuel a month, you could get back as much as $120 to use for things like building an emergency fund.

Why It's Essential to Eliminate Deadhead Miles

Deadhead miles refer to the distance you cover with an empty truck. The problem with this is that you still incur operating costs while no money comes into the business. So, deadhead miles are like somebody stealing money from your business. The trucking industry sees average deadhead miles of about 35% (Dalloo, 2019). Another problem with deadhead miles is that the truck is two and half times more likely to be involved in an accident tan with freight (Payne, 2016).

To avoid driving at a loss, deadhead miles might push you to charge higher freight rates. As such, you may not become deadhead miles price competitive and potentially lose customers. So, you need to have a strategy to circumvent deadhead miles.

One way is to use technology to your advantage. These tools help you match loads on a driver's route to eliminate deadhead miles. Other actions you may take include the following:

- Planning your loads ahead of time.
- Staying on schedule barring unforeseen circumstances. But even with this challenge, you could still communicate with shippers so that they could accommodate you.
- Bundle lanes with low and high volumes and offer shippers a discount. Try to at least get a higher freight rate than your cost per mile.

Running an Effective Collection Strategy

The trucking industry isn't a cash-based market. Instead, you deliver the freight, send an invoice, and get paid in 30, 60, or, in some extreme situations, 90 days. This means that you need to become skilled in cash collection. And that requires you to have a functional and effective collection strategy.

An ineffective strategy could result in cash flow problems, one of the major causes of business failures. With a sure-to-get-cash collection strategy, you'll free yourself to focus your energies on your core business of shipping loads. But a collection strategy doesn't work in isolation. It requires you to have sound contracts that specify exactly when the payment for the load is to be made. Furthermore, you should send clear and complete invoices with instructions on how your customers should pay you.

Here's what to consider when creating an effective collection strategy.

- **Run credit checks on your customers**. Doing this helps you to work with honest and reliable customers. All it requires is for you to run credit and background checks through inexpensive online services.

- **Create an invoice tracking system**. A system like this enables you to quickly detect overdue payments and act swiftly. Some systems are software-based. It's safer and cheaper to try free versions at the start of your business and upgrade as and when the need arises. If you want, you may start with a simple spreadsheet and build a few formulas to highlight invoices at different stages with specific color codes.

- **Eliminate prolonging payment terms**. Where possible, keep payments to 30 days during tough economic times. Offering an incentive like a discount could influence your customers to pay early. But ensure that you don't lose money in the process.

- **Invoice your customers as soon as you deliver the load**. There are invoicing apps that you can populate as soon as you deliver your customer's freight. This avoids payment excuses from some customers.

Now, after you get paid, you would like to access the funds as soon as possible. The way to do this is by signing up for functionalities like direct deposits or automated clearing house (ACH) transfers.

At times, it may become hard to access your cash when you desperately want it. As I explained earlier in the book, you could use any of the following avenues to access cash on short notice:

- Factoring.
- Business line of credit.
- Short-term loans.
- Business credit card.

However, use these sources sparingly because borrowing costs money, which, in turn, will affect your business profitability. Instead put more effort and time into your collection strategy as best as you can.

This chapter completes all that you need to know to start and build a thriving trucking business. The next section provides you with key ideas covered throughout the book.

Conclusion

Sometimes we read books and quickly forget the information and ideas that we got from them. That's why some people often read a book three, four, or five times. While reading a book, you find content and ideas that you know are useful. As a business consultant, I'm fortunate to understand what key concepts you may need to remind yourself about. And I included them in this chapter. The reason is to provide you with a quick resource you can use as a reference and save your time. But it will work for you only if you have read the book at least once. Here are the key ideas from this book.

A trucking company is an excellent business to start at present for several reasons. The trucking industry plays a significant role in moving goods throughout America. Up to around 72% of freight moves by road. A combination of the driver shortage, high freight demand, and increasing load prices is creating a demand for truck capacity. This presents an ideal opportunity to start a truck business. Furthermore, experts foresee the industry growing by a healthy 27% in the next decade. This offers a chance for business growth and an opportunity to grow your income as an owner.

Never start a trucking business without the right foundation and knowledge. It may be hard to start a trucking company, but the rewards are worth it. If you run your company well, you could profit around 7% of the business revenue. As you become more knowledgeable, skilled, and experienced, you could see your income swell to $100,000 or more per year. But even as a beginner, making income in the vicinity of $35,000 a year is not unheard of.

Part of running a successful trucking business involves creating a sound business plan. This working document forces you to think through the whole business startup process. Importantly, it guides your every move as you grow the business. That way, you may overcome mistakes that 85% of start-up trucking businesses make and fail.

If you want to run a legal business, you should register it with the government. You can choose your type of business entity between a sole proprietor, partnership, and limited liability company (LLC). I recommend organizing an LLC because you keep your personal and business assets separate. This is an excellent way to protect yourself or your business in the vent of a lawsuit.

The next vital legal aspect of a trucking business start-up is to get all the necessary licenses and permits. These will help you comply with various federal, state, or local laws. That way, you can operate your business with peace of mind. The key registration you must do is with the FMCSA to ensure you comply with trucking safety rules. And to obtain an operating authority so you can be paid for hauling freight. Don't forget to register for the necessary taxes, such as income, IFTA fuel, and sales tax. Remember that not all states charge income tax or gross receipts tax. Importantly, ensure you buy business insurance to cover liabilities in case events beyond your control occur.

It's impractical to try to run a trucking business without the right kind of vehicles. You can obtain these trucks by buying them outright or leasing them. And you can choose to either get new or used trucks. The key, though, is to ensure you purchase or lease mechanically sound vehicles. If you choose to lease, ensure that you select the right type. However, buying advantages you on the tax front. To make an informed decision, do a financial analysis of both leasing and buying.

If you choose to buy trucks, there are funding options available such as commercial truck financing, SBA loans. This is where your business plan and track record becomes vital. So, make sure that you have them.

Trucking is about moving loads from their sources to their destinations. Hence, you need to have drivers to operate the trucks. Even if you are an owner-operator, you still need to hire at least one driver to swap time off. So, having an ineffective recruitment strategy will go a long way to helping you hire the right kind of drivers. At the center of your truck driver hiring process should be finding employees with impeccable safety records.

Most importantly, it's vital to know how to find customers. They're the lifeblood of your business. Many strategies are available, including online marketing and personal prospecting. Running a business calls for negotiating skills. They'll help you win better-paying loads.

Finally, a business cannot succeed without sound financial management. You need to know the meaning of accounting terms like assets, liabilities, the cash flow statement, and the income statement. It is this accounting knowledge that's helpful when you analyze the profitability of your business. Most importantly, you need to manage the cash flow of your business. That's why you should have a cash-collection strategy.

I'm sure the knowledge and ideas you gained in this book will excite you to start your trucking business. There's no better time to become your own boss than now. Don't only read the book and let the knowledge sit in your mind without benefiting you and your loved ones. Go out there and apply what you've learned.

In conclusion, if you've found this book invaluable to your business knowledge, I would highly appreciate it if you could leave a glowing review.

References

Akalp, N. (2015, April 2). *How much does it cost to incorporate in each state?* Small Business Trends. https://smallbiztrends.com/2015/04/much-cost-incorporate-state.html

American Petroleum Institute. (2020, July). *Diesel tax.* www.Api.org. https://www.api.org/oil-and-natural-gas/consumer-information/motor-fuel-taxes/diesel-tax

American Trucking Associations. (n.d.). *Economics and industry data.* American Trucking Associations. https://www.trucking.org/economics-and-industry-data

Boyers, B. (2020, January 6). *How to apply for IFTA license and decals.* KeepTruckin. https://keeptruckin.com/blog/how-to-apply-ifta-license-decals

CDL.com. (n.d.). *How to start a trucking company [Your go-to guide].* CDL.com. https://www.cdl.com/trucking-resources/experienced-truck-drivers/how-to-start-trucking-company

Commercial Carrier Journal. (2019, October). *New research shows top reasons drivers leave within 90 days.* Commercial Carrier Journal. https://www.ccjdigital.com/new-research-shows-top-reasons-for-driver-turnover-within-90-days/

Corporation Service Company. (n.d.). *Start a trucking company in eight steps.* Corporation Service Company. https://www.incorporate.com/learning-center/start-trucking-company-eight-steps/

Dalloo, C. (2019, December 18). *Eliminating deadhead miles in trucking.* DriverSource. https://www.driversource.net/2019/12/18/eli minating-deadhead-miles-in-trucking/

Della Rosa, J. (2020, September 29). *Trucking industry strength has 'staying power,' might last years, reports show.* Talk Business & Politics. https://talkbusiness.net/2020/09/trucking-industry-strength-has-staying-power-might-last-years-reports-show/

DOT Federal Highway Administration. (2020, June 23). *What is the HVUT and who must pay it?* Department of Transport Federal Highway Administration. https://www.fhwa.dot.gov/policyinformation/ hvut/mod1/whatishvut.cfm

Driving Tests. (2020, June 13). *How to get a Commercial Driver License in 2020.* Driving Tests. https://driving-tests.org/how-to-get-a-cdl-license/

Federal Motor Carrier Safety Administration. (2019, December 16). *Insurance filing requirements.* Federal Motor Carrier Safety Administration. https://www.fmcsa.dot.gov/registration/insura nce-filing-requirements

Federal Motor Carrier Safety Administration (FMCSA). (n.d.). *Applying for USDOT number and operating authority.* Federal Motor Carrier Safety Administration. https://www.fmcsa.dot.gov/faq/applying-usdot-number-and-operating-authority

Freightos. (n.d.). *The beginner's guide to trucking: LTL Vs. FTL And other key trucking concepts.* Freightos. https://www.freightos.com/freight-resources/the-beginners-guide-to-trucking-ltl-vs-ftl-and-other-key-trucking-concepts/

Getloaded. (n.d.). *Starting a trucking company.* Www.Getloaded.com. http://www.getloaded.com/get-authority/how-to-start-a-trucking-business

John, S. (2019, June 3). *11 incredible facts about the $700 billion U.S. trucking industry.* Business Insider; Business Insider. https://markets.businessinsider.com/news/stocks/trucking-industry-facts-us-truckers-2019-5-1028248577

Motorcarrier HQ. (2019, November 11). *Understanding the UCR process and fees.* Motorcarrier HQ. https://www.motorcarrierhq.com/2015/07/14/understanding-the-ucr-process-and-fees/

Murray, J. (2020, May 22). *How can I get a Qualified Business Income deduction?* The Balance Small Business. https://www.thebalancesmb.com/how-can-i-get-a-qualified-business-income-deduction-4690835

PAM Transport. (n.d.). *Why we have one of the best truck lease purchase programs.* PAM Transport. https://pamdrivingjobs.com/why-we-have-one-of-the-best-truck-lease-purchase-programs/

Payne, R. (2016, February 3). *Empty trucks increase accident risk.* Phys.org; Science X Network. https://phys.org/news/2016-02-trucks-accident.html

PENSKE. (n.d.). *Lease vs buy a truck.* PENSKE. https://www.pensketruckleasing.com/full-service-leasing/leasing-benefits/lease-vs-own/

Randall-Reilly, & Commercial Carrier Journal. (2019). *What Drivers Want II.* Randall-Reilly. https://www.ccjdigital.com/wp-content/uploads/sites/10/2019/12/CCJ-What-Drivers-Want-Report-2019-2020-2019-12-04-10-14.pdf

Raphelson, S. (2018, January 9). *Trucking industry struggles with growing driver shortage.* NPR. https://www.npr.org/2018/01/09/576752327/trucking-industry-struggles-with-growing-driver-shortage

Resnick, R. (n.d.). *Setting up your business to receive payments.* Entrepreneur. https://www.entrepreneur.com/article/64838

Roadmaster Drivers School. (n.d.). *How much money do truck drivers make?* Roadmaster Drivers School. https://www.roadmaster.com/how-much-money-do-truck-drivers-make/

Rodela, J. (2018, October 23). *How much does it cost to start your trucking business?* KeepTruckin. https://keeptruckin.com/blog/cost-starting-trucking-business

Scott, A. (2018, October 27). *10 steps to setting up a limited liability company (LLC).* The Balance Small Business. https://www.thebalancesmb.com/how-to-set-up-a-limited-liability-company-llc-1200859

STANDARD CARRIER ALPHA CODE (SCAC) APPLICATION. (n.d.). https://emanifestcentre.com/wp-core/wp-content/uploads/2010/06/SCAC-APPLICATION2.pdf

Trucking Job Finder. (n.d.). *Trucking laws and regulations.* Trucking Job Finder. https://www.truckingjobfinder.com/members/info/trucking-laws/

Made in the USA
Columbia, SC
12 December 2022

73490247R00093